FORTY DREAMS
OF
ST. JOHN BOSCO

*"Amen I say to you, as long as you
did it to one of these my least brethren,
you did it to me."* —Matthew 25:40

St. John Bosco 1815-1888
Founder of the Salesian Order
The Apostle of Youth

FORTY DREAMS
OF
ST. JOHN BOSCO
THE APOSTLE OF YOUTH

From the Biographical Memoirs of
St. John Bosco

Compiled and Edited by
Fr. J. Bacchiarello, S.D.B.

*"But they that are learned shall shine as
the brightness of the firmament: and they that
instruct many to justice, as stars for all
eternity."* —Daniel 12:3

TAN BOOKS AND PUBLISHERS, INC.
Rockford, Illinois 61105

Nihil Obstat: E. Gutierrez, S.D.B.
                 August 21, 1969

Imprimatur: ✠ Stephen Ferrando, S.D.B., D.D.
               Bishop of Shillong, India
               September 21, 1969

This book was previously published in approximately 1969, in India, and printed at the Salesian Institute of Graphic Arts, Madras.

Re-typeset and re-published by TAN Books and Publishers, Inc. in 1996 with permission of Most Rev. Joseph Aind, now Bishop of Dibrugarh (Assam), and by arrangement with Salesiana Publishers, New Rochelle, New York.

Library of Congress Catalog Card No.: 96-61323

ISBN 0-89555-597-2

Printed and bound in the United States of America.

Cover picture of St. John Bosco and Boys of the Oratory reproduced by permission of Fr. Aurelius Maschio, S.D.B.

TAN BOOKS AND PUBLISHERS, INC.
P.O. Box 424
Rockford, Illinois 61105
1996

"The teacher who is seen only in the classroom, and nowhere else, is a teacher and nothing more; but let him go with his boys to recreation and he becomes a brother."

(*Page* 219)

CONTENTS

ACKNOWLEDGMENTS

For the English translation of the dreams selected from Volumes I-IX and XI we are deeply indebted to Very Rev. Father Diego Borgatello and his collaborators in the translation of the *Biographical Memoirs* from the Italian. The volumes are a real monument, "more lasting than bronze," erected to our saintly Father, Don Bosco.

The Biographical Memoirs can be obtained from:
    Salesiana Publishers
    130 Main Street
    New Rochelle, N.Y. 10801

Some of these dreams have been reprinted from pamphlets published by the Salesian House of Tirupattur (North Arcot); others are from Father Motta's books printed by Tang King Po School (Hong Kong); others are new translations. Don Bosco's vision of St. Dominic Savio is copied from a translation by Rev. Father Terence O'Brien, S.D.B. in his book *Dominic Savio, Teenage Apostle,* Part II: Appendix.

For greater details about Don Bosco's dreams, consult the chapter on "Dreams, Visions and Ecstasies" in Fr. Ceria's book *Don Bosco with God.*

.

PREFACE TO THE 1969 EDITION

Dear Readers,

This second edition of *Dreams of Don Bosco* comes to you ten years after the first edition, which went out of print seven years ago.

At the request of many friends, I have revised and enlarged this new volume by the addition of many more dreams of special interest and utility to you.

A word about the dreams of Don Bosco: God spoke to Don Bosco in dreams. Who would ignore *dreaming of dreams* which the prophet Joel counts among the gifts that were to gladden, by a generous effusion of the Holy Spirit, *the latter days,* that is, as St. Peter explains, the days of the Messias? (*Acts* 2:17). Don Bosco's hearers gathered more than 150 dreams.

Some of Don Bosco's dreams are prophetic, others are pedagogical, and some are parables. Some concern the Church, some the nations, others the Salesian Congregation, the missions, the Oratory (the first Salesian institution), etc.

Most of Don Bosco's dreams are certainly supernatural events. Here are some proofs:
1. Sometimes he said that "it was a dream in which one can know what one does; can hear what is said, can ask and answer questions." This does not happen in ordinary natural dreams.
2. He usually had a guide and interpreter. Who was he? Sometimes Dominic Savio or Louis Colle or an Angel, or St. Francis de Sales, or someone else. Their explanations are always precise and instructive. This does not happen in usual dreams.
3. Often he saw the secret things of conscience, and the test proved it always to be true; the foreseen future events (includ-

ing deaths) did actually occur. This Don Bosco considered *"an extraordinary grace granted for the benefit of all the children of the Oratory."*

4. Don Bosco used to narrate his dreams with a very great spirit of humility, thinking only of the spiritual benefit of his hearers. The good effects were evident: especially a greater horror for sin, better Confessions, General Confessions, more frequent Communions. It was, as he sometimes put it, *"The Devil's Bankruptcy."*

5. In natural dreams there is no logical order. All the opposite happens in the dreams of Don Bosco. Images and words are so well connected that one seems to hear things seen with open eyes.

6. Don Bosco's dreams contained clear and exact revelation of events to come. As many prophecies as he had made of all kinds of things came about before or after his death. Innumerable examples can be read in the *Biographical Memoirs* (twenty large volumes).

7. On the 17th of February, 1871, Don Bosco candidly told some Salesians that *"these things are certainly singular and must be spoken of only among ourselves (in the Salesian House), because if they were told to anyone outside, these people would certainly dub them as fables. But we have always this as our norm that, when something turns out to the good of our souls, it certainly comes from God, not from Satan."*

In the 11th volume of the *Biographical Memoirs,* page 239, we read: "Don Bosco's dreams had become like a 'domestic institution' at the Oratory. The expectation of new dreams was ever present. News of another dream aroused anticipation among young and old alike: its narration was eagerly listened to; its salutary effects were not long in coming."

May the reading of the following selection of dreams bring even now similar benefits.

God be with you.

FR. JOSEPH BACCHIARELLO, S.D.B.
SAVIO JUNIORATE
MAWLAI, SHILLONG - 793008

FORTY DREAMS
OF
ST. JOHN BOSCO

"And I will give you pastors accord-
ing to my own heart, and they shall feed
you with knowledge and doctrine."
—Jeremias 3:15

THE FIRST DREAM

1

(*Biographical Memoirs*, Vol. I, page 94)

John Bosco, born in 1815, passed his earliest years in the happy liberty of the fields of Becchi, a small village in Piedmont, Italy. As a little shepherd boy, he would play with his young companions, drawing them away from evil and leading them on to virtue.

In 1823 he wanted to go to school in the town of Castelnuovo, a few miles away; but his ignorant twenty-year-old stepbrother prevented him, because he wanted hands to work in the fields and vineyard.

But during the winter of 1824-1825, when in Piedmont there is no work in the snowy fields, John Bosco's mother sent him to school in a nearby village. There a priest of great piety taught him to read and write, and above all taught him his catechism and prepared him for his first Confession. Under the guidance of this priest, the young John Bosco learned the means necessary for preserving God's grace in the soul by *prayer and mortification.*

Once able to read, John would often be seen with a book in hand, even while watching the animals in their pasture. On one occasion, some other shepherd boys wanted John to join their games, but he refused and they beat him. He might have paid them back. But forgiveness was his revenge. He told them: "I cannot play, because I must study; I want to become a priest."

After that, they left him in peace. Admiring his patience

and meekness, they became his friends, and so John Bosco would instruct them in catechism and teach them to sing hymns to our Blessed Mother.

Then, when John Bosco was nine years old, he had a dream which revealed to him his future vast and providential mission for boys during his laborious life. He himself narrates this dream in his *Memoirs of the Oratory*.

John Bosco wrote his *Memoirs of the Oratory of St. Francis de Sales* after an explicit order from the Holy Father. After a short preface to the manuscript for his Salesians, he narrates the following dream:

Part I. Jesus Commands

When I was about nine years old, I had a dream that left a profound impression on me for the rest of my life. I dreamed that I was near my home, in a very large playing field where a crowd of children were having fun. Some were laughing, others were playing and not a few were cursing. I was so shocked at their language that I jumped into their midst, swinging wildly and shouting at them to stop. At that moment a Man appeared, nobly attired, with a manly and imposing bearing. He was clad with a white flowing mantle, and His face radiated such light that I could not look directly at Him. He called me by name and told me to place myself as leader of those boys, adding these words:

"You will have to win these friends of yours not with blows but with gentleness and kindness. So begin right now to *show them that sin is ugly and virtue beautiful*."

Confused and afraid, I replied that I was only a boy and unable to talk to these youngsters about religion. At that moment the fighting, shouting and cursing stopped, and the crowd of boys gathered around the Man who was talking. Almost unconsciously, I asked:

"But how can you order me to do something that looks so impossible?"

"What seems so impossible you must achieve by being *obedient* and by *acquiring knowledge*."

"But where? How?"

"I will give you a Teacher under whose guidance you will learn and without whose help all knowledge becomes foolishness."

"But who are you?"

"I am the Son of her whom your mother has taught you to greet three times a day."

"My mother told me not to talk to people I don't know, unless she gives me permission. So please, tell me your name."

"Ask My Mother."

Part II. Mary, His Teacher

At that moment I saw beside Him a Lady of majestic appearance, wearing a beautiful mantle, glowing as if bedecked with stars. She saw my confusion mount, so she beckoned me to her. Taking my hand with great kindness, she said:

"Look!"

I did so. All the children had vanished. In their place I saw many animals: there were goats, dogs, cats, bears and a variety of others.

"This is your field; this is where you must work," the Lady told me. "Make yourself humble, steadfast and strong. And what you will see happen to these animals you will have to do for my children."

I looked again; the wild animals had turned into as many lambs—gentle, gamboling lambs—bleating a welcome for that Man and Lady.

At this point of my dream, I started to cry, and I begged the Lady to explain what it all meant, because I was so utterly confused. She then placed her hand on my head and said:

"In due time everything will be clear to you."

After she had spoken these words, some noise awakened me; everything had vanished. I was completely bewildered.

St. John Bosco's first dream-vision, which took place when he was nine
years old. In this dream, Our Lord called John Bosco to teach young boys
that virtue is beautiful and sin is ugly. Our Lord also promised to give His
Mother to John Bosco as a guide and helper.

Somehow my hands still ached and my cheeks still stung because of all the fighting. Moreover, my conversation with that Man and Lady so disturbed my mind that I was unable to sleep any longer that night.

In the morning I could barely wait to tell my dream. When my brothers heard it, they burst out laughing. I then told my mother and grandmother. Each one who heard it gave it a different interpretation. My brother Joseph said:

"You're to become a shepherd and take care of goats, sheep and livestock."

My mother's comment was: "Who knows? Maybe you will become a priest."

Dryly, Anthony muttered: "You might become the leader of a gang of robbers."

But my very religious, illiterate grandmother had the last word: "You mustn't pay attention to dreams."

I felt the same way about it, yet I could never get that dream out of my head. What I am about to relate may give some new insight into it. I never brought up the matter and my relatives gave no importance to it. But in 1858, when I went to Rome to confer with the Pope about the Salesian congregation, Pius IX asked me to tell him everything that might have even the slightest bearing on the supernatural. Then, for the first time, I told him the dream that I had had when I was nine. The Pope ordered me to write it in detail for the encouragement of the members of the Congregation, for whose sake I had gone to Rome.

This dream came back to John Bosco over and over again for a period of eighteen years; but with each repetition there were always many new additions. With each new vista, he was able to envision more clearly not only the establishment of his Oratory and the spread of his work, but also the obstacles that were to arise, the stratagems of his enemies and the way to overcome them.

JOHN BOSCO DREAMS THE MONTHLY TEST 2

(*Biographical Memoirs*, Vol. I, page 190)

During his high school years, John Bosco, in addition to his intelligence and memory, had yet another talent, which was extraordinary and very valuable. Here is one of many incidents:

One night John dreamed that his teacher had given a monthly test to determine class rank and that he was taking this test. The moment he awoke, he jumped out of bed and wrote out the test, which was a Latin passage, and began translating it with the assistance of a priest who was a friend of his. Believe it or not, that very morning the teacher did give a test, and it was the same Latin passage John had dreamed about! Thus, quite quickly and without needing a dictionary, he translated it as he had done after waking from his dream. Of course, the result was excellent. When the teacher questioned him, he candidly told him what had happened, to the teacher's amazement.

On another occasion, John handed in his test so quickly that the teacher seriously doubted that the boy could have managed all its grammatical problems in such a short time. So he went over John's test very carefully. The teacher had prepared that test only the night before. It had turned out rather lengthy and therefore the teacher had dictated only half of it: yet in John's composition book the test was written out in its entirety, to the last word! How could it be explained?

John could not have copied it overnight, nor could he possibly have broken into the teacher's house, which was a considerable distance from where John lived. What then? He confessed: "I dreamed it!" It was for this reason that his schoolmates nicknamed him "The Dreamer."

THE DREAM OF THE SHEPHERDESS

3

(*Biographical Memoirs*, Vol. II, page 190)

John Bosco was ordained on June 5, 1841. The sacred ministry was the ideal of his whole life; the long-desired goal had finally been attained. He was twenty-six years old. He spent the first few months of his priesthood in his native Castelnuovo, with his beloved pastor, Father Cinzano. About those months, we read the following in his memoirs:

In that year, 1841, since my pastor was without an assistant, I served as one for five months. I found great pleasure in this work. I preached every Sunday, visited the sick and administered the Sacraments, but I did not hear Confessions, as I was not yet authorized to do so. I conducted funeral services, kept the parish records in order and issued certificates as required. But my greatest delight was teaching catechism to the children, passing the time with them and talking to them. They often came from Murialdo to visit me, and whenever I walked home, they thronged around me. Also in Castelnuovo the youngsters began to make friends with me and seek my company. Whenever I left the rectory, I was escorted by a crowd of boys, who followed me wherever I went.

Don Bosco had three offers of appointment with generous stipends. In order to understand God's will, he went to Turin to seek the advice of Fr. (now St.) Joseph Cafasso, his spiritual guide, who was a lecturer at the *Convitto Ecclesiastico*, an institution for the training of young priests in pastoral life. Fr. Cafasso advised him to enroll at the *Convitto Ecclesiastico*. It was from there that Don Bosco began his Sunday Catechism for poor children on December 8, 1841. For several years it was a wandering Oratory; nobody wanted to be disturbed by the shouts of hundreds of boys at play. So Don Bosco and his boys had to change location several times. (Cf. *Biographical Memoirs*, Vol. 2, Ch. 6 and 7.) But a wonderful dream disclosing future events came to him and comforted him. Let us narrate this dream in his own words from the pages of his memoirs:

On the second Sunday of that year (1844), I was to tell my boys that the Oratory[1] was being transferred to the Valdocco area. I was, however, truly worried because I was uncertain about the exact location, the means and the people to help me. On Saturday night I had a new dream, which seemed to be a sequel to the one I had had at Becchi when I was about nine years old. I think it best to put it down literally.

I dreamed that I was in the midst of a multitude of wolves, goats, kids, lambs, sheep, rams, dogs and birds. The whole menagerie raised an uproar, a bedlam, or better, a racket that would have frightened even the bravest man. I wanted to run away, when a Lady dressed as a shepherdess beckoned me to follow her and accompany the strange flock she was leading.

We wandered aimlessly, making three stops along the way, at each of which many of those animals changed into lambs, so that the number of lambs continually increased. After a long trek, I found myself in a meadow, where those animals

---

1. Don Bosco called his Sunday gatherings of boys "Oratory," i.e., a place of prayer, because of its primary purpose, namely, to teach them to go to church and pray. Its objectives were the practice of religion and virtue, the boys' moral education and, consequently, the salvation of their souls. Recreation, entertainment, singing and schooling, which followed in due time, were only the means. (For more information about this, see Volume 2, Chapters VII and XI of *Biographical Memoirs*.)

St. John Bosco's dream of the Shepherdess (Our Lady), who pointed out his vocation to educate and care for boys.

were grazing and frolicking, making no attempt to bite each other.

I was exhausted and wanted to sit by the roadside, but the Shepherdess invited me to keep walking. A short distance away, I came upon a large playground surrounded by porticoes, with a church at one end. Here I noticed that four-fifths of those animals had become lambs. Their number was now very large. At that moment many young shepherds came to watch over them, but they remained only a short time and walked off. Then a marvelous thing happened . . . many lambs turned into shepherds, and they took care of the flock. When the shepherds became too many, they parted and went elsewhere to herd other strange animals into pens.

I wanted to leave, because I thought it was time for me to say Mass, but the Shepherdess asked me to look to the south. On doing so, I saw a field in which maize, potatoes, cabbage, beets, lettuce and many other vegetables had been planted. "Look again," she said. I did so, and I beheld a monumental church. In the choirloft I saw choristers and musicians who seemed to be inviting me to sing Mass. On a white streamer inside the church there was emblazoned in large letters: *HIC DOMUS MEA; INDE GLORIA MEA*—"This is my house; from here my glory will go forth." Still dreaming, I asked the Shepherdess where I was and the meaning of all this walking, the stops, that house, the church and then another church. "You will understand everything," she answered, "when with your bodily eyes you will behold all that you now see in your mind." I thought I was awake, and so I said, "I see clearly, and with my bodily eyes; I know where I am going and what I am doing." Just then the bell of St. Francis of Assisi Church rang the "Ave Maria" and I awoke.

The dream lasted nearly the whole night, and there were many other details. At the time I understood little of it because, distrusting myself, I put little faith in it. As things gradually began to take shape, I began to understand. In fact, later on, this dream, together with another, formed the basis of my planning while at the Rifugio.

THE FUTURE OF THE ORATORY

4

(*Biographical Memoirs*, Vol. II, page 232)

St. John Bosco had another comforting dream, or better, a series of dreams, when he was ordered to vacate the quarters lent for the Oratory at the "Rifugio" of Marchioness Barolo. This is how he narrated it in 1875 to some Salesian priests:

Youngsters Fighting

I seemed to be in a vast meadow with a huge crowd of boys who were fighting, swearing, stealing and doing other blameworthy things. The air was thick with flying stones, hurled by youngsters who were fighting. They were all abandoned boys, devoid of moral principles. I was about to turn away when I saw a Lady beside me. "Go among those boys," she said, "and work."

I approached them, but what could I do? I had no place to gather them, but I wanted to help them. I kept turning to some people who were watching from a distance and who could have come to my aid, but no one paid attention or gave me any assistance. I then turned to the Lady. "Here is a place," she said, and pointed to a meadow. "That's only a meadow," I said.

She replied: "My Son and His Apostles did not even have a place to lay their heads." (Cf. *Matt.* 8:20). I began to work in that meadow, counselling, preaching, hearing Confessions, but I saw that almost all my efforts were in vain. I had to have some building where I could gather and house those abandoned by their parents and those despised and rejected by society. Then the Lady led me a little farther to the north and said: "Look."

The Churches—The Martyrs

I did so and saw a small church with a low roof, a small courtyard and a great number of boys. I resumed my work, but since the church was becoming too small, I again appealed to the Lady, and she pointed out another church, much larger, and a house adjacent to it. Then she took me closer to a field that was tilled and that lay almost opposite the façade of this new church. "In this place," she added, "where the glorious martyrs of Turin, Adventor and Octavius suffered martyrdom, on these clods soaked and sanctified by their blood, I wish that God be honored in a very special manner." So saying, she put out her foot and pointed to the exact spot where the martyrs had fallen. I wanted to leave a marker there so as to find the place again when I returned, but I could not see a single stick or stone. Nevertheless, I kept the place clearly in mind. It coincides exactly with the inner corner of the chapel of the Holy Martyrs, previously known as St. Anne's Chapel; it is the front left corner as one faces the main altar of the Church of Mary, Help of Christians.

In the meantime, I found myself being surrounded by a vast and ever-increasing number of boys, but as I kept looking to the Lady, the premises and the means were also growing accordingly. I then saw a very grand church on the exact spot she had pointed out as the place where the soldiers of the Theban legion had been martyred. There were a great many buildings all around, and in the center stood a beautiful monument.

The Ribbon of Obedience

While these things were taking place and I was still dreaming, I saw that priests and clerics were helping me; but after a while, they left. I tried everything to get others to stay, but after a while, they too left me alone. Then I turned once more to the Lady for help. "Do you want to know what to do to keep them?" she asked. "Take this ribbon and bind their foreheads with it." Reverently, I took the white ribbon from her hand and noticed the word OBEDIENCE written on it. I immediately gave it a try and began to bind the foreheads of these volunteers. The ribbon worked wonders. As I went ahead with the mission entrusted to me, all my helpers gave up the idea of leaving me, and stayed on. Thus was our Congregation born.

I saw a great many other things, but there is no need to relate them now. Suffice it to say that ever since, I have walked on sure ground as regards the Oratories, the Congregation and the manner of dealing with outsiders, irrespective of their position. I have already foreseen all the difficulties that will arise, and I know how to overcome them. I can see perfectly, bit by bit, what is to take place, and I go forward without hesitation. It was only after I had seen [in dreams] churches, schools, playgrounds, boys, clerics and priests helping me and I had learned how to advance the entire apostolate, that I began to mention it to others and speak of it as a reality. That is why so many people thought that I was talking foolishly and believed I was insane.[1]

---

1. Cf. Vol. II, page 319 and Vol. XV of *Biographical Memoirs.*

THREE
MARTYRS

5

(*Biographical Memoirs*, Vol. II, page 268)

The Wandering Oratory

For the first five years (1841-1846), Don Bosco's Oratory was a "wandering oratory" (cf. *Biographical Memoirs* Vol. 2, 262ff). Either because the premises were not large enough for hundreds of boys at play, or because the neighbors were disturbed, he had to move with his flock from place to place, persecuted by some, admired and helped by others. But Our Lady consoled and guided him in all these wanderings.

One of his dreams unveiled to him yet another marvelous sight. He disclosed this briefly and only to a few intimates in 1884, but its most striking aspects escaped his lips on various occasions, whenever, during a span of twenty years, he would gaze with great emotion and almost ecstatically upon the Church of Mary, Help of Christians. We at his side treasured his words and carefully jotted them down each time, and then we were able to reconstruct his dream as follows:

Don Bosco seemed to be at the northern edge of the "Rondo" or Valdocco circle. Looking towards the Dora River, along the tall trees which at that time lined the boulevard now known as Corso Regina Margherita, he happened to see, about two hundred feet away, near the present Via Cottolengo, three handsome youths, resplendent with brilliance. They were standing in a field then planted with potatoes, maize, beans and cabbage, and they stood precisely on the spot which in a previous dream had been pointed out to him as the place

St. John Bosco with "Mama Margarita" (his mother) and "Grigio"—the miraculous dog that would appear out of nowhere when St. John Bosco needed protection. Mama Margarita became a devoted mother to the many boys in St. John Bosco's care.

where the three soldiers of the Theban Legion had gloriously suffered martyrdom. They gestured to him to come and join them. Don Bosco hurried over and, with great kindness, they took him to the farther end of that field, where the majestic Church of Mary, Help of Christians now stands.

Mary Reassures Him

During that brief walk, Don Bosco saw wonder upon wonder, and finally he stood before a Lady remarkably beautiful and majestic, splendidly clothed, around whom stood venerable men who resembled a senate of princes. Hundreds of people in glittering array formed her retinue as though she were queen; and other similar throngs were visible as far as the eye could see. The Lady beckoned Don Bosco to draw near. When he was close to her, she told him that the three young men who had accompanied him were the three martyrs Solutor, Adventor and Octavius, and he interpreted this to mean that they would be the Patron Saints of that place.

Then, with an enchanting smile and affectionate words, she encouraged him never to abandon his boys, but to carry on the great work he had begun with even more determination. She informed him that he would encounter many serious obstacles, but that they would all be overcome and swept aside by his firm faith in the Mother of God and her Divine Son.

Finally, she pointed out to him a house which really did exist and which he later found out belonged to a man named Pinardi. She also showed him a small church on the same spot where the Church of St. Francis de Sales and its adjacent buildings now stand. She then raised her right hand and in an infinitely melodious voice said: *HAEC EST DOMUS MEA; INDE GLORIA MEA*—"This is my house; from here my glory will go forth." On hearing these words, Don Bosco was so moved that he woke up. The Blessed Virgin, for truly this was she, and the entire vision faded slowly from view as the mist at dawn.

St. John Bosco's dream of Mary, Help of Christians, surrounded by the three martyrs Solutor, Adventor and Octavius, as well as a host of other Saints. The Latin words *Hic domus mea; inde gloria mea* translate, "This is my house; from here my glory will go forth."

THE FUTURE CHURCH OF ST. FRANCIS DE SALES **6**

(*Biographical Memoirs*, Vol. II, page 318)

Difficulties never deterred Don Bosco from his resolve: this was a lifetime trait of his. Once he had reached a decision, after long reflection and consultation with his superiors and other prudent people, he never withdrew until he had completed his task. But he started nothing from purely human motives. While asleep, he was favored with visions that offered enlightenment. These he narrated to Father Michael Rua and others in the first years of his work.

Sometimes he would find himself gazing upon some buildings and a church, the whole complex identical to the present Oratory of St. Francis de Sales (the Mother House of the Salesian Society).[1] On the façade of the church there was the legend: *HAEC EST DOMUS MEA; INDE GLORIA MEA—* "This is my house; from here my glory will go forth." Boys, seminarians and priests were coming and going through its portals. This vision sometimes gave way to another. In the same place there would appear the little Pinardi House, and around it porticoes adjoining a church, and a large number of boys, clerics and priests. "But this can't be," Don Bosco told himself. "That is too good to be true. Is this a diaboli-

---

1. In the following pages, the word "Oratory" means Don Bosco's first boarding school in the district of Valdocco in Turin. It began as a "Festive Oratory," but then the name was equally applied to the boarding establishment added to the Festive Oratory, also called the "Mother House."

cal illusion?" Then he distinctly heard a voice saying to him: "Do you not know that the Lord can enrich His people with the spoils of the Egyptians?" (Cf. *1 Mach.* 1:20.)

At other times he seemed to be in Via Cottolengo. On his right there stood the Pinardi house, in the midst of a vegetable garden, surrounded by fields; on his left, almost opposite the Pinardi house, was the Moretta house with the adjacent playgrounds and fields, where the Daughters of Mary, Help of Christians were later to establish themselves. Two pillars stood at the main gate of the future Oratory of St. Francis de Sales, and over them Don Bosco could read the following inscription: *HINC INDE GLORIA MEA*—"From here and from there my glory will go forth." This was evidently the first intimation of a sister congregation which was to flourish beside the Salesians. If he saw the latter, is it not likely that he also saw the sisters? Be it as it may, he was sparing with words in these matters, so he said nothing at that time.

Meanwhile, the first dream (Vol. II, p. 190f) he had had at the Convitto was about to be verified. Don Bosco was to make three stops before finding a permanent residence. The first had been at the Rifugio,[2] and the second at the Molini Dora. The Moretta house[3] with its "meadow" was to be the third. May God be blessed.

---

2. "Rifugio" or "Pia Opera del Rifugio" ("Pious Work of the Refuge") was one of the many charitable institutions opened and endowed by Marchioness Barolo. It included the St. Philomena Hospital. When Don Bosco was appointed assistant Chaplain at the Rifugio, he was allowed to use for his Festive Oratory some rooms of the St. Philomena Hospital, which had not yet been opened. (Cf. *Biographical Memoirs* Vol. II, Ch. 4.)

3. Moretta (Casa): a house at Valdocco where Don Bosco rented rooms for evening and Sunday classes for the Oratory when he had to leave the Rifugio. (Cf. *Biographical Memoirs* II, Ch. 37.)

TWO BOYS ATTACKED BY A MONSTER

7

(*Biographical Memoirs*, Vol. II, page 396)

Don Bosco had this dream when convalescing at home in Becchi after a serious illness. The number of Oratory boys was then 629. During his absence Father Borel and other helpers ran the Festive Oratory. (Cf. Vol. II, pages 380-399.)

There were only two cases in which Don Bosco could not remain unperturbed: when souls were in danger or were lost, and when God was offended.

Around that time, Joseph Buzzetti told us Don Bosco had a dream which made him very unhappy. He saw two boys, whom he recognized, leave Turin to come to visit him; but when they came to the bridge over the Po, a horrible and repulsive creature attacked them. After it had slobbered all over them, it flung them to the ground, dragging them for some distance through the mud, so that they were covered with filth from head to foot. Don Bosco told this dream to several of the boys staying with him, mentioning the names of the boys he had seen in the dream. Subsequent events proved the dream to be something more than mere imagination, because those two unfortunate boys abandoned the Oratory and gave themselves up to a dissolute life.

DEADLY NOOSES 8

(*Biographical Memoirs*, Vol. IX, page 278)

I dreamed that I walked out of my room and instantly found myself in church. It was packed full with the pupils of the Oratory, Lanzo and Mirabello, as well as many youngsters unknown to me. The boys were not praying aloud, but seemed to be preparing for Confession. I observed a very large number crowding around my confessional beneath the pulpit, and I began to wonder how I could possibly hear them all. I suspected that I might be dreaming. To make sure I was awake, I clapped my hands and distinctly heard the noise they made. To be sure beyond question, I stretched out my hands and felt the wall behind my confessional. With no room for doubt, I said to myself: "I might as well start." And so I began hearing Confessions. Soon, concerned about the number of boys, I got up to see if there were any other confessors, but there were none, so I made for the sacristy, hoping to find help. It was then that I noticed that some boys had a noose around their necks which nearly choked them.

"What is that rope for?" I asked. "Take it off." In reply they just stared at me.

"You," I said to a youngster, "go to that boy and slip that noose off his neck."

The boy went, but came back, saying: "I can't get it off. Someone is holding it. Come and see."

Ugly Cats

I scrutinized that huge crowd of boys more closely and thought I saw two very long horns jutting out behind many of them. I got closer to the one nearest me and, drawing up behind him, I saw a hideous cat tightly clinging to the noose. Surprised in the act, it tried to crouch lower and hide its snout between its paws. I asked this boy and the others their names, but they did not answer. I questioned that frightful beast, but it only crouched lower.

"Go to the sacristy and ask Father Merlone for the holy water," I directed one of the boys.

He soon returned with it, but meanwhile I discovered that behind each boy crouched a cat as hideous as the first one. I continued to hope that it was a dream. Seizing the sprinkler, I turned to one of those large cats.

"Tell me who you are," I ordered.

Alternately opening and closing its jaws, the hideous animal broke into a growl and prepared to lunge.

"Answer me!" I insisted. "What are you doing here? I do not fear your rage. Do you see this holy water? I will thoroughly soak you with it."

In dismay the monster began to writhe in unbelievable contortions and again seemed ready to leap at me. I kept my eye on it and noticed that it was holding several nooses in its paw.

"What are you doing here?" I asked again, while threatening it with the holy water. The monster then relaxed its taut position in order to run away.

"Stop!" I demanded. "You stay right here!"

"Look then," it growled and showed me its nooses.

"What are they? What do you mean?" I asked.

"Don't you understand? I rope these boys into making bad Confessions. With these nooses I drag nine-tenths of mankind into Hell."

"Then in the name of Jesus Christ, speak!"

Writhing hideously, the monster answered: "With the first

noose I make the boys conceal their sins in Confession."

"And with the second?"

"I make them confess without true sorrow."

"And with the third?"

"I won't tell you."

"You had better tell, or you'll be drenched with this holy water!"

"No, no, I will not! I've talked too much already!" And it growled in fury.

"Tell me so that I can inform the directors of our schools," I demanded, raising the sprinkler.

Flames and even a few drops of blood darted from the beast's eyes as it grudgingly muttered: "With the third noose I keep them from making a firm resolution and carrying out their confessor's advice."

"You hideous beast," I exclaimed. I wanted to question the monster further, and force it to tell how I could remedy this great evil and offset its diabolical efforts, but all those hideous cats, which until now had done their utmost to stay hidden, began to mutter and then broke out into loud shouts against the one which had spoken. Amid the general uproar, I realized that I could get nothing more from the monster. Therefore, lifting the sprinkler and flinging holy water upon the one who had spoken I commanded, "Go away," and it disappeared. Then I sprinkled holy water all about, and in the pandemonium which ensued, all those cats scurried away. The din awakened me, and I found myself in bed.

Sincerity—Sorrow—Resolution

My dear boys, I would never have thought that so many of you had nooses around your necks. You know what they stand for. The first noose shames a boy into concealing sins in Confession or lying about the number of times—for instance, accusing himself of committing a sin three or four times when it was exactly four times. This is just as insincere as concealing sins. The second stands for lack of sorrow, and the third for lack of firm resolution. If we are to rid ourselves of these nooses and wrench them from the devil's clutches, let us confess all our sins and be truly sorry for them.

Shortly before flying into rage, the monster told me: "See how much good boys draw from Confession! If you want to know whether or not I hold them in leash, see if they are becoming better."

I also forced the devil to tell me why he was crouching behind your backs. "So that I can't be seen," it replied. "That way it is easier for me to drag them down into Hell." Those of you who had those monsters behind their backs were far more numerous than I would have believed.

Make what you will of this dream, but it is a fact that I did check on these things and found that what I had dreamed was quite true. Let us, therefore, take advantage of this opportunity of gaining a plenary indulgence by making a good Confession and Communion. Let us do our utmost to free ourselves of the devil's nooses.

On the occasion of the Golden Jubilee of his ordination, the Holy Father granted a plenary indulgence to all those who on next Sunday, April 11, after receiving the Sacraments, will pray for his intention. This coming Saturday, Chevalier Oreglia will have a private audience with the Holy Father and will offer him an album bearing your signatures and those of the boys attending our schools and oratories. In the meantime, see whether your past Confessions were well made. I will remember you all in my Holy Mass next Sunday.

THE PARTRIDGE AND THE QUAIL

9

(*Biographical Memoirs*, Vol. 8, page 9)

I will now tell you a dream I had the night before last. I was hiking with all of you and many others whom I did not know. We stopped in a vineyard for refreshment, and everyone scattered about to pick fruit, feasting on grapes, figs, peaches and plums. I was with you, plucking grapes and figs for you to eat.

I seemed to be dreaming and somehow regretted that it was only a dream. "Anyhow," I said to myself, "let the boys have their fill." Through the rows of vines, we could see the vinedresser.

Once we had our fill, we resumed our march through the vines, but we had a hard time crossing the deep furrows running the whole length of the vineyard. The sturdier boys managed to jump from one row to the other; the smaller ones could not quite make it and usually tumbled into a deep furrow. Sympathizing with their plight, I looked about for some other way out and noticed a dirt road alongside the vineyard. I made for it with all of you, but the vinedresser stopped me. "Listen to me," he said. "Keep off that road. It's rocky, miry, thorny and rutted—absolutely impossible. Stay on the path you have taken."

"I'd like to," I replied, "but these little fellows cannot make it across the furrows."

"That's no problem." he countered. "Let the bigger boys carry the younger ones. They will still be able to jump from row to row."

Unconvinced, I made for the dirt road with all the boys, only to find that it was indeed forbidding and impassable. Turning to Father Francesia, I remarked: "We are between the devil and the deep blue sea." We had no choice but to keep crossing those furrows along a path parallel to the dirt road. When we finally reached the last row of vines, we were faced by a thick hedge of thorns. Clearing a passage with great difficulty, we descended a lofty bank into a lush, tree-dotted meadow.

In its center I spotted two former Oratory pupils who, on recognizing me, came over to greet me. We chatted for a while. Then, one of them, holding up two birds, said, "See what I found! Aren't they cute?"

"What are they?" I asked.

"This one is a partridge and this a quail!"

"Is the partridge alive?"

"Sure!" And he placed a most beautiful fledgling into my hands.

"Can it feed itself?"

"Yes, it has just started." While watching it eat, I noticed that is beak was split into four parts. Surprised, I asked the boy about it.

"You mean you don't know?" he replied. "The four parted beak symbolizes the same thing as the partridge itself."

"I don't understand."

"You should! After all, you are well educated. What is the Latin word for partridge?"

"Perdix."

"Well, then, you have it!"

"I still don't understand! Tell me."

"All right, I will. Consider what each letter stands for:

'P': *Perseverantia*—'Perseverance.'

'E': *Æternitas te expectat*—'Eternity awaits you.'

'R': *Referet unusquisque secundum opera sua prout gesit: sive bonum, sive malum*—'Everyone must render an account of his deeds, whether good or evil.'

'D': *Dempto nomine*—'Without regard to his name, worldly

fame, glory, knowledge or wealth.'

'I': *Ibit*—'He shall go.' Now you also know what the four-parted beak means: The Four Last Things.

"I see—but what does 'X,' the last letter, stand for?

"Can't you guess? Didn't you study mathematics?"

"All right! 'X' stands for an unknown quantity."

"Good! Now replace the word quantity with destiny and you have 'Unknown destiny.' *Ibit in locum suum*—'He shall go to his unknown destiny.'

Amazed, but also convinced by this explanation, I asked him, "May I keep this partridge?"

"You are welcome to it," he replied. "Would you like to look at the quail too?" He added.

"Yes, let me see it."

He handed it to me. It seemed to be a very fine looking bird, but on lifting its wings I saw it was covered with sores. [The more I examined it,] the more hideous, festering and foul smelling it became.

"What happened?" I asked the lad.

"You are a priest and have studied Holy Scripture, and yet you don't understand? Don't you remember that when the Israelites grumbled in the desert, God sent them a flock of quails? The Israelites feasted on them, but even as they ate, God punished thousands of them. This quail tells you that gluttony is more deadly than the sword, and it is the fountainhead of most sins."

I thanked him for this explanation.

Meanwhile, a large number of other partridges and quails appeared over all the hedges, trees and meadow. You boys pounced upon them and got yourselves a meal. We then resumed our march. Those who had fed on partridges felt strong and followed me; those, instead, who had feasted on quails lingered in the valley and scattered about. I saw them no more.

On January 18, Don Bosco spoke thus to the boys:

I know you would like to hear more about the dream I told you the other night. I will only disclose what the partridge and quail stand for. In brief, the partridge stands for virtue and the quail for vice. I need not tell you that the fine looks of the quail masking the putrid sores under its wings symbolize impurity. The boys greedily feasting on quail, notwithstanding its rotten condition, are those who give themselves to sinful habits, while the lads eating partridge are those who love and practice virtue.

I saw boys holding a quail in one hand and a partridge in the other, but feeding exclusively on quail. These lads know the beauty of virtue, but refuse to use the God-given means to become good. Others, instead, fed on partridge, but kept glancing longingly at the quail. They are those who walk the path of virtue, but halfheartedly, by force. Unless they change their outlook, sooner or later they will fall.

I also noticed that quails would keep fluttering in front of boys eating partridge, but these lads just ignored them. These are the ones who follow virtue and who loathe and despise vice. Then there were boys who ate both partridge and quail. These are the fellows who swing from vice to virtue and vice-versa, fooling themselves into believing that they are not so bad after all.

"Who of us was eating what?" you may ask. I have told many yesterday. As for the rest, let them come to me and I'll tell them too.

What shall we say now about the above-narrated dream? Don Bosco, as was his wont, did not explain it fully, limiting himself to what concerned the boys and to some insights into the future. Yet, if we are not mistaken, on studying his words we see in his dream the Oratory, the Salesian society and religious orders in general.

The partridge: Smartness is a trait of this bird. Cornelius à Lapide, in fact, commenting on Chapter 17 of Jeremias, quotes St. Ambrose (Letter 47) where he describes the smart and often successful tricks of the partridge to escape the hunter's snares and save its brood. One of Don Bosco's frequent sayings to his pupils was: "Be smart!" The inference was that the thought of eternity would suggest to them how to escape the devil's snares.

The quail: Symbol of impure things. Also: *gluttony kills vocations*.

THE PRECIOUS HANDKERCHIEF OF PURITY

10

(*Biographical Memoirs,* Vol. VI, page 582)

This dream of the handkerchiefs warns us to be quick in reacting against impure temptations. To remain dilly-dally would lead one into sin. Who can put out the fire when all the house is in flames?

Does the wind of temptation blow? Turn at once to the right, namely, turn to Mary for help. Those imprudent boys who kept their handkerchiefs of the Queen of Virtues exposed to the wind, the rain and the hailstones soon found them riddled with holes, shapeless and without any beauty.

One of the men who were near the Lady (perhaps a minister of God) shouted: "Turn RIGHT." Nearly all obeyed and turned to the right: that is, they made good Confessions. So they repaired their handkerchiefs. But the handkerchiefs, though patched, had no more regular shape. God forgives, but nature punishes! Habits of impurity will always have bad consequences. Only time, good will and the grace of God can repair the damages. One must cultivate piety, humility, a spirit of sacrifice and do good works for the love of Jesus Christ. Those who continue in bad habits run great risk of eternal damnation.

Here is the summary of the talk Don Bosco gave on June 18, 1861, about the precious handkerchiefs:

On the night of June 14, I had no sooner fallen asleep than I was startled by a heavy blow on the bedstead, as if someone had struck it with a board. I jumped up and immediately thought that it was lightning. I looked around, but found nothing unusual. Convinced that I had most likely been dreaming, I again tried to sleep. Hardly had I begun to doze when a second blow startled me again. This time I got out of bed and searched everywhere—under the bed, under the desk and in the corners of the room—but I found nothing amiss. Commending myself to God's safekeeping, I blessed myself with holy water and slipped into bed. It was then that my mind began to wander, and I saw what I am going to tell you.

An Immense Valley

I seemed to be in our church pulpit, about to start a sermon. All the boys were seated in their usual places, looking up and waiting, but I had no idea what to preach about. My mind was a complete blank. For a while I stood there dumbfounded and dismayed. Never had anything like this happened to me in all the years of my ministry. Then suddenly the walls and the boys disappeared, and the church turned into an immense valley. I was beside myself and could not believe my eyes. "What's this?" I questioned. "A moment ago I was in the pulpit in church and now I am in a valley. Am I dreaming? What's happening to me?"

I decided to get going, hoping to meet someone and find out where I was. After a while, I came to a stately palace. Its many balconies and broad terraces beautifully harmonized with the building and the landscape. In front of the palace there was a large plaza. In a corner, at the right, many boys were crowding around a Lady who was handing out handkerchiefs, one to each boy. On taking theirs, the boys walked up to the terrace and ranged themselves along the parapet. Drawing close to the Lady, I heard her say to each lad as she gave him a handkerchief: "Do not unfold it when it is windy, but if you are surprised by wind, turn at once to the right, never to the left."

The Storm

I kept looking at those boys, but then and there I did not recognize any of them.

When all the handkerchiefs had been distributed, the boys were all lined up on the terrace in complete silence. As I watched, one boy took out his handkerchief and unfolded it. Others followed his example, and soon all had them out. The handkerchiefs were very large and exquisitely embroidered in gold. On each, lengthwise, there was written in gold: *Regina Virtutum*—"Queen of Virtues."

Suddenly, a soft breeze came out of the north—that is, from the left. Gradually it grew stronger; then it became a wind. Some of the boys immediately folded their handkerchiefs and hid them, while others turned quickly to the right. Others instead, left them exposed and flapping in the wind. Meanwhile, the disturbance gained force, while ominous clouds gathered overhead and darkened the sky. Lightning flashed and thunderous frightening rumbles rolled across the heavens, followed by hail, rain and snow. Unbelievably, many boys still kept their handkerchiefs flapping in the storm. The hail, rain and snow battered them mercilessly. In no time they were riddled with holes, torn beyond recognition.

I was stunned, not knowing what to make of it. However, I was in for a still greater shock. As I got closer to the boys for a better look, I recognized every one of them. They were my own Oratory boys. I hurried up to one of them and asked, "What in the world are you doing here? Aren't you so-and-so?"

"Yes," he replied, "I am." And then, pointing to several others, he added, "So-and-so and so-and-so are here too!"

I then went over to the Lady who had distributed the handkerchiefs. Several men were around her.

"What does all this mean?" I asked them.

The Lady herself, hearing my question, turned to me. "Did you not see the inscription on those handkerchiefs?" she asked.

"Why, yes, my Lady," I replied: "*Regina virtutum.*"

"Do you understand now?"
"Yes, I do!"

Prompt Recourse to Prayer

All those boys exposed their purity to the wind of temptation. Some, on realizing the danger, immediately fled. Those are the boys who folded and hid the handkerchiefs. Others, taken by surprise and unable to fold their handkerchiefs, turned to the right. These are the boys who promptly have recourse to prayer when in danger and turn their backs upon the enemy. Others, instead, kept their handkerchiefs open to the full blast of temptation and fell into sin.

Saddened by this sight and the realization that so very few of my boys had kept themselves pure, I nearly burst into tears. When I was able to control myself again, I asked, "Why did even raindrops and snowflakes riddle the handkerchiefs? Aren't they symbols of venial sin?"

One of the men replied: "Don't you know that where purity is concerned, *non datur parvitas materiae*—'there is no matter that is not considered to be grave'? Nevertheless, don't be downhearted; come and see."

He moved to the balcony and, signaling to the boys with his hand, shouted, "Right about face!" Nearly all obeyed; but a few did not budge. Their handkerchiefs were torn to shreds. I noticed too that the handkerchiefs of those who had turned to the right had shrunk and were covered with patches. They had no holes, but were pitifully shapeless.

"These boys," the Lady explained, "had the misfortune of losing their purity, but they regained God's grace through Confession. Those few who did not stir are those who persist in sin and perhaps will go to perdition." Finally, she said to me: *"Nemini dicite, sed tantum admone"*—"Tell no one in particular, but give only a general warning."

A
HORNED
CAT

11

(*Biographical Memoirs*, Vol. 8, pp. 20 & 25)

Two or three nights ago I had a dream. Would you like to hear it? You are very dear to me, and so you are always in my dreams. I seemed to be in the playground with you swarming around me. Each one held a rose, a lily, a violet, or both a rose and a lily, or some other flower. Suddenly, a huge, ugly cat, black as coal, appeared. It had horns, eyes as red as live coals, long sharp claws and a disgustingly swollen belly. This ugly beast edged stealthily close to you and swiftly clawed your flowers to the ground. When I first spotted this hideous creature, I was terrified, but to my astonishment you seemed totally unconcerned. Seeing it creep towards me to knock my flowers down, I immediately turned to dash off, but someone stopped me. "Don't run away," he said. "Hasten to tell your boys to raise their arms up high beyond the beast's reach."

I did as he told me. The monster tried hard to jump up, but its weight made it fall back clumsily to the ground.

The lily, my dear sons, symbolizes the beautiful virtue of purity, against which the devil wages endless war. Woe to those who keep their flower low! The devil will snatch it from them. Such are those who pamper their flesh by overeating or eating between meals, who shirk work and idle away their time, who are fond of certain conversations or books and who shun self-denial . . . For goodness' sake, my children, fight this enemy or it will enslave you.

These victories are hard to win. But Holy Scripture tells us the means to use: "This kind (of devil) can be cast out only by prayer and fasting." (*Matt.* 17:20). Raise your arm, and your flower shall be safe. Purity is a heavenly virtue. Whoever wishes to safeguard it must raise himself heavenward. Prayer is your salvation. By prayer I mean your morning and night prayers devoutly said, meditation and Holy Mass, frequent Confession and Communion, sermons and exhortations, visits to the Blessed Sacrament, the Rosary and your school duties. By prayer you will rise heavenward. Thus you will safeguard the most beautiful of virtues. Try as much as he wants, the devil will not be able to snatch it from you.

(For more comments by Don Bosco, one may read a long "Good Night" address on pp. 25-28 of the same Vol. 8, 1865, February 6 and 13.)

A
FIENDISH
ELEPHANT

12

(*Biographical Memoirs*, Vol. VII, page 212)

As of January 1, 1863, the Society of St. Francis de Sales had thirty-nine members, including Don Bosco. Most of them were young clerics, of whom twenty-two had consecrated themselves to God with triennial vows. There were six priests: five professed and one without vows.

Don Bosco began the new year by appealing to the public for financial help. The lottery proceeds, though substantial, could not provide for the construction of the new wing along via della Giardiniera, the maintenance of the Oratory boarders and the realization of other major projects which Don Bosco had been planning for some time. First on the mailing list were cabinet ministers, the royal family and their almoner, Fr. Camillo Pelletta of Cortanzone.

Don Bosco still owed his boys the yearly *strenna*,[1] and at the same time he felt he had to reveal to them something extraordinary for their spiritual welfare. The deaths he had predicted at the end of the year had reformed many hearts, but not all. A number of new pupils and a few old ones still refused to make their peace with God and went on living thoughtlessly in spite of God's wondrous mercy. "Good and

---

1. A New Year's gift customary in Italy. From the very beginning of the Oratory, Don Bosco had started the custom of giving a spiritual *strenna* or gift to his boys and co-workers on the last day of the year. It took the form of a motto or slogan to be practiced in the year then about to dawn. This custom is still kept by Don Bosco's successors.

upright is the Lord," says the psalmist: *"He shows sinners the way, He guides the humble to justice, He teaches the humble His way."* (*Ps.* 24:8-9). This we have already seen and shall continue to see.

Since he had not been able to give the annual strenna to his pupils on the last day of the year, Don Bosco promised to do so on the evening of the Feast of the Epiphany. Therefore, on Tuesday, January 6, 1863, after the night prayers, as all artisans and students eagerly awaited him, Don Bosco mounted the platform and addressed them:

Tonight I should give you the strenna. Every year around Christmas I regularly beg God to suggest a strenna that may benefit you all. In view of your increased number, I doubled my prayers this year. The last day of the year (Wednesday) came and went, and so did Thursday and Friday, but nothing came to me. On Friday night, January 2, I went to bed exhausted, but could not fall asleep. The next morning I arose from bed worn out and almost half dead, but I did not feel upset over it. Rather, I was elated, knowing from past experience that a very bad night is usually a forewarning that Our Lord is about to reveal something to me. That day I went on with my work at Borgo Cornalese; the next day, by early evening, I arrived back here. After hearing Confessions, I went to bed. Tired from my work at Borgo and from not sleeping the night before, I soon dozed off. Now began the dream which will give you your strenna.

The Enormous Elephant

My dear boys, I dreamed that it was a feast day afternoon and that you were all busy playing, while I was in my room with professor Thomas Vallauri (a contemporary lexicographer, prominent literary man and dear friend of Don Bosco) discussing literature and religion. Suddenly, there was a knock at my door. I rose quickly and opened it. My mother—dead now for six years—was standing there. Breathlessly, she gasped, "Come and see! Come and see!"

"What happened?" I asked.

"Come! Come!" she replied.

I dashed to the balcony. Down in the playground, surrounded by a crowd of boys, stood an enormous elephant.

"How did this happen?" I exclaimed. "Let's go down!"

Professor Vallauri and I looked at each other in surprise and alarm and then raced downstairs.

As was only natural, many of you had run to the elephant. It seemed meek and tame. Playfully it lumbered about, nuzzling the boys with its trunk and cleverly obeying their orders, as though it had been born and raised at the Oratory. Very many of you kept following it about and petting it, but not all. In fact, most of you were scared and fled from it to safety. Finally, you hid in the church. I too tried to get in through the side door which opens into the playground, but as I passed Our Lady's statue beside the drinking fountain and touched the hem of her mantle for protection, she raised her right arm. Vallauri did likewise on the other side of the statue, and the Virgin raised her left arm. I was amazed, not knowing what to think of such an extraordinary thing.

The Enemy of the Eucharist

When the bell rang for church service, you all trooped in. I followed and saw the elephant standing at the rear by the main entrance. After Vespers and the sermon, I went to the altar, assisted by Fr. Alasonatti and Fr. Savio, to give Benediction. At the solemn moment when you all deeply bowed to adore the Blessed Sacrament, the elephant—still standing at the end of the middle aisle—knelt down too, but with its back to the altar.

Once services were over, I tried to dash out to the playground and see what would happen, but I was detained by someone. A while later, I went out through the side door which opens into the porticoes and saw you at your usual games. The elephant too had come out of the church and had idled over to the second playground where the new wing is under construction. Mark this well, because this is precisely the place where the grisly scene I am going to describe occurred.

At that moment, at the far end of the playground, I saw a banner followed processionally by boys. It bore in huge letters the inscription *Sancta Maria, succurre miseris!*—"Holy Mary, help your forlorn children!" To everybody's surprise, that monstrous beast, once so tame, suddenly ran amuck. Trumpeting furiously, it lunged forward, seized the nearest boys with its trunk, hurled them into the air or flung them to the ground and then trampled them underfoot. Though horribly mauled, the victims were still alive. Everybody ran for dear life. Screams and shouts and pleas for help rose from the wounded. Worse—would you believe it?—some boys who were spared by the elephant, rather than aid their wounded companions, joined the monstrous brute to find new victims.

Under Her Mantle

As all this was happening (I was standing by the second arch of the porticle, near the drinking fountain), the little statue that you see there (the statue of the Blessed Virgin) became alive and grew to life-size. Then, as Our Lady raised her arms, her mantle spread open to display magnificently embroidered inscriptions. Unbelievably, it stretched far and wide to shelter all those who gathered beneath it. The best boys were the first to run to it for safety. Seeing that many were in no hurry to run to her, Our Lady called aloud, *"Venite ad me omnes!"*—"Come all to me!" Her call was heeded, and as the crowd of boys under the mantle increased, so did the mantle spread wider. However, a few youngsters kept running about and were wounded before they could reach safety. Flushed and breathless, the Blessed Virgin continued to plead, but fewer and fewer were the boys who ran to her. The elephant,

St. John Bosco's dream of The Fiendish Elephant, which, representing the devil, hurled boys into the air or flung them to the ground and them trampled them underfoot. Only those boys were saved who took shelter under the mantle of Mary. (The elephant is at the far left of this picture.)

41

meanwhile, continued its slaughter, aided by several lads who dashed about, wielding one sword or two and preventing their companions from running to Mary. The elephant never even touched these helpers.

Meanwhile, prompted by the Blessed Virgin, some boys left the safety of her mantle in quick sorties to rescue some victims. No sooner did the wounded get beneath Our Lady's mantle than they were instantly cured. Again and again several of those brave boys, armed with cudgels, went out and, risking their lives, shielded the victims from the elephant and its accomplices until nearly all were rescued.

The playground was now deserted, except for a few youngsters lying about almost dead. At one end by the portico, a crowd of boys stood safe under the Virgin's mantle. At the other stood the elephant with some ten or twelve lads who had helped it wreak such havoc and who still insolently brandished swords.

Suddenly rearing up on its hind legs, the elephant changed into a horrible, longhorned specter and cast a black net over its wretched accomplices. Then, as the beast roared, a thick cloud of smoke enveloped them, and the earth suddenly gaped beneath them and swallowed them up.

Promises and Maxims

I looked for my mother and professor Vallauri to speak to them, but I could not spot them anywhere. Then I turned to look at the inscriptions on Mary's mantle and noticed that several were actual quotations or adaptations of Scriptural texts. I read a few of them:

> *Qui elucidant me vitam aeternam habebunt*—"They that explain me, shall have life everlasting." (*Ecclus.* 24:31).
> *Qui me invenerit, inveniet vitam*—"He who finds me, finds life." (*Prov.* 8:35).

Si quis est pravulus, veniat ad me—"Whoever is a little one, let him come to me." (*Prov.* 9:4).
Refugium peccatorum—"Refuge of sinners."
Salus credentium—"Salvation of believers."
Plena omnis pietatis, mansuetudinis et misericordiae—"Full of piety, meekness and mercy."
Beati qui custodiunt vias meas—"Blessed are they that keep my ways." (*Prov.* 8:32).

Avoid Foul Talk

All was quiet now. After a brief silence, the Virgin, seemingly exhausted by so much pleading, soothingly comforted and heartened the boys and, quoting the inscription I had inscribed at the base of the niche, *Qui elucidant me, vitam aeternam habebunt,* she went on:

"You heeded my call and were spared the slaughter wrought by the devil on your companions. Do you want to know what caused their ruin? *Sunt colloquia prava:* Foul talk and foul deeds. You also saw your companions wielding swords. They are those who seek your eternal damnation by enticing you from me, just as they did with some schoolmates of yours.

But *quos Deus ditius exspeciat durius damnat*—"those for whom God keeps waiting, He punishes more severely." The infernal demon enmeshed and dragged them to eternal perdition. Now, go in peace, but remember my words: Flee from companions who befriend Satan, avoid foul conversation, have boundless trust in me. My mantle will always be your safe refuge."

Our Lady then vanished; only her beloved statuette remained. My deceased mother reappeared. Again the banner with the inscription, *Sancta Maria, succurre miseris*, was unfurled.

Marching processionally behind, the boys sang *Laudate Maria, O lingue fideli*—"Praise Mary, O ye faithful tongues." Shortly afterwards, the singing waned and the whole scene faded away. I awoke in a sweat. Such was my dream.

My sons, now it is up to you to draw your own strenna. Examine your conscience. You will know if you were safe under Mary's mantle, or if the elephant flung you into the air, or if you were wielding a sword. I can only repeat what the Virgin said: *Venite ad me omnes*—"Come all to me." Turn to her; call on her in any danger. I can assure you that your prayers will be heard. Those who were so badly mauled by the elephant are to learn to avoid foul talk and bad companions; those who strive to entice their companions from Mary must either change their ways or leave the house immediately. If anyone wants to know the role he played, let him come to my room and I will tell him. But I repeat: Satan's accomplices must either mend their ways or go! Good night!

Don Bosco had spoken with such fervor and emotion that for a whole week afterward the boys kept discussing that dream and would not leave him in peace. Every morning they crowded his confessional; every afternoon they pestered him to find out what part they had played in the mysterious dream.

That this was no dream, but a vision, Don Bosco had himself indirectly admitted when he said: "I regularly beg God to suggest . . . A very bad night is usually a forewarning that Our Lord is about to reveal something to me." Furthermore, he forbade anyone to make light of what he had narrated.

But there is more. On this occasion he made a list of the wounded and of those who wielded one or two swords. He gave it to Celestine Durando, instructing him to watch them. The cleric handed the list over to us, and it is still in our possession. The wounded were thirteen—probably those who had not been rescued and sheltered beneath Our Lady's mantle. Seventeen lads wielded one sword; only three had two. Scattered marginal notes next to a boy's name indicate an amendment of life. Also, we must bear in mind that the dream, as we shall see, referred also to the future.

That it mirrored the true state of things was admitted by the boys themselves:

"I had no idea that Don Bosco knew me so well," one of them stated. "He revealed my spiritual condition and my temptations so exactly that I could find nothing to add."

Two other boys were told that they were wielding swords. "It's quite true," each admitted. "I knew it all along." They mended their ways.

One afternoon, while talking of this dream and remarking that some boys had already left the Oratory and others would soon follow, lest they harm their companions, Don Bosco came to mention his own "wizardry," as he called it. In this connection he told the following incident:

Some time ago, a boy wrote home and falsely accused priests and superiors of the house of grave wrongdoings. Fearing that Don Bosco might see the letter, he held on to it till he could secretly mail it. That same day, right after dinner, I sent for him. In my room I told him of his misdeed and asked why he had told such lies. Brazenly, he denied everything. I let him talk, and then word for word, I repeated the contents of the letter to him. Embarrassed and frightened, he knelt at my feet in tears. "Was my letter intercepted?" he asked.

"No," I replied. "Your family has probably received it by now, and it's up to you to put matters right."

The boys around him asked how he had found that out. "Oh, it's my wizardry," he answered with a laugh. This wizardry and his dream, which revealed not only the boys' present spiritual condition, but their future as well, must have been one and the same thing.[2]

---

2. For further comments one may read pages 217-220 of Vol. VII.

DEATH'S MESSENGER   **13**

(*Biographical Memoirs*, Vol. VII, page 76)

On March 21, 1862, Don Bonetti's chronicle records, Don Bosco mounted his little platform to give the "Good Night" address to the boys. After a few moments silence, as if to catch his breath, he began:

I must tell you a dream. Try to picture to yourselves the Oratory at recreation time, loud with happy, boisterous youngsters. I seemed to be leaning out of the window of my room, watching the boys joyfully playing their games, running and dashing about the playground. Suddenly, I heard a loud disturbance at the main entrance. I looked and saw a tall old man; he had a wide forehead, oddly sunken eyes, a long white beard and white locks thinly falling about his shoulders. He was draped in a winding sheet, which he clutched tightly in his left hand, while in his right he held a dark blue flaming torch. He advanced slowly and gravely, halting at times to search stoopingly, as if trying to find a lost object; unseen, he wandered about the entire playground several times, while the boys went on with their games.

Dumbfounded and puzzled, I kept watching him. He went up to the carpenter shop, halted before a boy who was playing *barra rotta* (a sort of cops-and-robbers game) and, extending a lanky arm, held the torch up to the lad's face. "He's the one, I'm sure," he muttered and brusquely nodded two or three times. Then abruptly he cornered the boy and handed him a note from the folds of his winding sheet.

Taking it, the boy unfolded it and visibly paled as he read
it.

"When?" he asked. "Soon?"

"Now," was the ghastly reply.

"Can't I finish the game?"

"You may be caught while you are playing."

It meant a sudden death. Trembling, the boy tried to say
something, to plead, but somehow could not. Unclutching his
robe, the stranger then pointed to the portico with his left
hand: "Look," he said. "Do you see that coffin? It's for you!
Quick, let's go!" In the center of the passageway leading into
the orchard lay a coffin.

"I'm not ready . . . I'm still too young to die!" the boy
screamed. Silently, the stranger quickly strode away.

As I tried to learn who he was, I woke up. From what I
have said, you may well understand that one of you must prepare himself, because the Lord will soon call him into eternity. I know who he is, because I saw the whole thing. I
know the boy to whom the stranger handed the note. He is
here now listening to me, but I shall tell no one till after his
death. However, I will do all I can to prepare him for a happy
death. Let each of you look after himself, for while he wonders who it is, he himself may be just the one. I have told
you this because if I failed to do so, the Lord would ask me:
"Why do you not speak up at the proper time?" So let each
one correct himself, especially during these last three days of
the novena before the Feast of the Annunciation. Pray especially for this purpose and, during these three days, say at
least one "Hail, Holy Queen" to the Blessed Virgin for the
boy who has to die. When he departs from this life, our several hundred prayers will greatly help him.

The Bonetti Chronicle continues:

When Don Bosco stepped down, some asked him privately
to tell them at least if that boy would die soon. He replied
that this would unfailingly happen before two feast days beginning with the letter "P" and perhaps even before the first of

those feasts; it might be two or three weeks.

This dream caused shudders; everyone feared he might be the one. As on previous similar occasions (see Vol. VI, pp. 484-89—"Consciences revealed"), it did a lot of good. Each one took heed of his spiritual welfare, and on the following day the boys went to Confession in greater numbers than usual.

For several days many lads personally tried to get Don Bosco to tell them their fate, but they kept asking in vain. Two things stood out very clearly in their minds: Death would be sudden, and it would occur before two solemn feast days beginning with the letter "P"—obviously Pasqua (Easter) and Pentecost. The first fell on April 20.

There was a great hubbub at the Oratory on April 16, 1862, when a twelve-year-old boy, Louis Fornasio of Borgaro Torinese, died at home. There are several things to be said about him. When Don Bosco announced that one of the boys was to die, this lad, though by no means bad, began to be a model of good behavior. The first four days after the announcement he pestered Don Bosco to let him make a General Confession. Reluctant at first, because the youngster had already made one before, Don Bosco finally relented as a special favor and heard his Confession in two or three different sessions. Moreover, on the same day that he had asked for the favor, or on the day when he started his Confessions, the youngster began to feel slightly sick, and this condition persisted for the next few days. At this juncture, two of his brothers came to visit him and, seeing that he was ill, got Don Bosco's permission to take him home for awhile. On this very day—or the day before—Fornasio had finished his General Confession and had also received Holy Communion. He went home with them, was on his feet for a few days, but then had to take to bed. His illness soon took a turn for the worse, affecting his brain and depriving him of speech and at times of his consciousness. Of course, he could not make his Confession or receive Communion. When Don Bosco, a good father, paid him a visit, Fornasio recognized him and tried to say something, but after vain efforts, he broke into sobs, while his whole family wept with him. He died the following day.

When this news reached the Oratory, several clerics asked Don Bosco whether Fornasio was the boy of the dream. Don Bosco gave them to understand that he was not. Nevertheless, several believed that this boy's death had fulfilled the prediction. At the "Good Night" address that same evening, April 16, Don Bosco announced Fornasio's death, remarking that it taught them all an important lesson: "Make hay while the sun shines," he said. "Let us not allow the devil to delude us into thinking we may put our conscience in order at the moment of death." When someone publicly asked him whether Fornasio was the boy destined to die, he replied that he would say nothing for the moment. He added, though, that it was usual at the Oratory for boys to die in pairs—one calling another—and that, therefore, we should still be on guard and heed Our Lord's advice: "Be ready, because at an hour that you do not expect, the Son of man will come." (*Matt.* 24:44).

When he descended from the platform, he said quite plainly to a few priests and clerics that Fornasio was not the boy of the dream.

On April 17, during after-dinner recreation, a crowd of boys kept pestering Don Bosco, "Tell us the name of the boy who is to die!" Smilingly, Don Bosco kept shaking his head, but they insisted, "If you don't want to tell us, then tell at least Fr. Rua." Don Bosco continued to shake his head.

"Just tell us his initial, then," several insisted.

"All right, I'll satisfy you in that," he replied. "He has the same initial as the name of Mary."

The disclosure spread like wildfire, but a guess was still difficult. More than thirty boys had surnames beginning with "M."

There were some skeptics too, because a boy named Louis Marchisio was seriously ill and there were grave fears for his life. In fact, the following day, April 18, he was taken home. These skeptics, guessing that Don Bosco had been alluding to him, remarked, "Well, we too can predict that someone whose name begins with 'M' is going to die!"

The Bonetti Chronicle continues (Vol. VII, pp. 81-83):

On Easter Sunday, April 29, 1862, Don Bosco became very ill. So weak was he that he could hardly stand on his feet or speak. Nevertheless, he left his room and heard Confessions from six-thirty until nine.

A month had gone by since the prediction, and the healthy apprehension it had generated was now waning. Yet many kept wondering, "Who will die and when? Pasqua—the first 'P'—is gone!"

Quite unexpectedly, on April 25, Victor Maestro of Viora, Mondovi, at the age of thirteen, died of a stroke. He was a very fine lad who went to Communion several times a week. To the very day of Don Bosco's prediction he was well, but two weeks before his death his eyes began bothering him and his vision dimmed in the evening. Two or three days before the stroke, he complained of slight chest pains, for which the doctor prescribed longer sleep.

One morning Don Bosco met him on the stairs. "Would you like to go to Heaven?" he asked.

"Of course," Maestro answered.

"Then get ready!" The boy was startled for a moment, but then thinking that Don Bosco had spoken in jest, he regained his composure. However, Don Bosco, keeping close to him for the next few days, prepared him properly and induced him to make a general, most consoling Confession.

On April 24, a boy noticed Maestro sitting on the infirmary balcony. Impulsively, he approached Don Bosco. "Is it true that Maestro is the boy who wants to die?" he asked.

"How would I know!" Don Bosco replied. "Ask him!"

The lad went up to the balcony and did just that. Maestro broke into a laugh and, going downstairs, asked Don Bosco to let him go home for a few days. "Surely," Don Bosco agreed, "but before you go, have the doctor give you a written report on your illness." The boy felt relieved. He had said to himself, *"Someone is to die at the Oratory. If I go home, it can't be me. I'll have a longer Easter holiday and come back in perfect shape."*

The next day, Friday, April 25, Maestro got up with the others and heard Mass; then, feeling quite tired, he returned to bed, after telling schoolmates how glad he was that he could go home.

When the bell rang for classes at nine, his friends wished him a happy vacation and a safe return, said goodbye and went to school. Maestro was left alone in the dormitory. Towards ten, the infirmarian looked in to tell him that the doctor was expected soon and that he should get up and report to the infirmary.

The doctor arrived shortly. A boy in the adjoining dormitory, who also had to see the doctor, went to Maestro's dormitory and called him loudly from the doorway. Hearing no answer, he called again. There was still no reply. Thinking that Maestro was sound asleep, he went to his bedside and shook him, calling his name. Maestro was motionless. Frightened beyond words, the lad screamed, "Maestro is dead!" and dashed out to call someone. The first one he met was Fr. Rua, who ran to Maestro's bedside in time to give him absolution as he died. Fr. Alassonatti, the prefect, was informed immediately, and Bonetti went to call Don Bosco.

The news spread like lightning through classrooms and workshops. Boys came running and knelt down in prayer. Others, hoping that Maestro might still be alive, brought bedwarmers and cordials to revive him, but it was all useless. On first sight Don Bosco knew the boy was dead. Everybody was heartbroken, particularly because Maestro had died with no friend by him. Knowing the boys' grief, Don Bosco assured them of Maestro's eternal salvation. He had received Communion on Wednesday, and since the Feast of All Saints he had especially behaved and was properly prepared for death. A steady flow of clerics and boys paid him their last respects. As they mourned him, they realized that his death had fulfilled Don Bosco's prediction.

That evening Don Bosco's "Good Night" address moved all to tears. He called attention to the fact that within the last nine or ten days God had taken two of our companions, and neither had had a chance to receive the last Sacraments. "How mistaken people are," he exclaimed, "to delay clearing their conscience till the end of their life. Let us thank the Lord for thus calling into eternity two companions who, we are sure, were spiritually ready. How much more would we grieve if others had been taken whose conduct is quite unsatisfactory."

Maestro's death was a blessing of the Lord. On Saturday morning and evening, boys in great numbers wanted to make a General Confession. With two or three words Don Bosco put their minds at ease. Later he said very plainly: "Maestro was the boy whom I saw receive the note in my dream . . . What deeply consoles me is that he went to the Sacraments that very Friday morning, as several boys have assured me. His death was sudden, but not unprovided."

Maestro's body was interred on the morning of Sunday, April 27. A remarkable incident fulfilled the prediction to the last detail. The mysterious stranger of the dream had handed a note to Maestro as he was standing in the portico facing the passageway leading to the orchard. From there he pointed out to the boy the coffin in the passageway only a few feet away.

When the undertaker and his assistants came, they carried the body down the central staircase, along the portico up to that passageway. There they stopped, sent for chairs and placed the coffin on them as they waited for the priest and students who were to escort the body to the cemetery.

(Thus reads the Bonetti chronicle.)[1]

We must point out too that John Cagliero (then a deacon), passing by, was distressed by this arrangement because, at other funerals, the coffin had customarily been set down at the far end of the portico near the door of the stairs adjoining the church. He was more displeased to learn that the morticians themselves had had the chairs removed from their customary place. He insisted that the coffin be placed at the usual spot, but the men gruffly refused.

---

1. Cf. Vol. VI, pages 339-431.

Just then Don Bosco came out of church. Looking very sadly upon the coffin, he remarked to John Baptist France-sia and others: "What a coincidence! That's the way I saw it in the dream!"

FIERCE CROWS AND A HEALING SALVE

14

(Biographical Memoirs, Vol. VII,
pages 391-393)

For over a month, the Ruffino chronicle tells us, Don Bosco suffered from a persistent eye ailment which forced him to wear dark glasses. Still, he kept working and urging his priests and young clerics to do likewise. "Courage," he said. "Let us work wholeheartedly for youth. Let us do all we can for God's glory and the welfare of souls. Up there a great reward awaits us, the same as promised to Abraham: 'I am . . . your reward exceeding great.' *(Gen.* 15:1). At times we may feel tired, exhausted or overwhelmed by ailments, but we must take heart, because up there we shall rest forever." And he would raise his right hand toward Heaven in a gesture of full trust in the Lord.

Wealth Is a Temptation

His co-workers often discussed with him the field of activities which Divine Providence would probably entrust to them. On one such occasion, April 3, 1864, the conversation shifted to the possibility of one day conducting a boarding school for the sons of noble families. "Oh, no," Don Bosco interrupted. "Not as long as I live! Never, if I can help it! If it were only a matter of administration, we might consider it. Not otherwise. It would ruin us just as it has ruined many illustrious religious orders who started out with the poor and ended up with the rich. The outcome was that they ran into envy, jealousy and attempts to supplant them. Wealth and hob-nobbing with the rich are common temptations. If we keep working for poor boys, we shall be left in peace, if for no other reason than that some will put up with us in pity and others will perhaps praise us. No one will covet our possessions. They wouldn't care for our rags."

The Retreat

On April 4, Don Bosco notified the boys that their annual spiritual retreat would start on April 11. The gist of his talk was this: "To make a good retreat, you must be prepared. Unless you start making definite plans now, your retreat will be only a flash in the pan. 'I will catch up on my sleep,' one may say, or 'I'll do my best to have a good time reading some interesting book or munching on something,' or 'I'll use my time to review some subject.' Others may say, 'I want to reap some spiritual fruit and think about my vocation.' This is the smart thing to do. What can we say of the others? What can we tell them? My dear boys, this retreat may very well be your last. Think of that!"

The retreat schedule was posted on April 11. It was the last time the artisans made their retreat with the students. Increased enrollment thereafter necessitated scheduling two separate retreats. The preacher was Fr. Ignatius Arro.

Confession

Don Bosco spent endless hours in the confessional. "In this ministry," Cardinal Cagliero states, "his kindness to young and old alike was exceptional, unwavering and admirable. Nearly all of us went to him for Confession because of his ever benign, patient gentleness and charity. He was more indulgent than severe and encouraged us to trust in God's mercy, while he inspired God's holy fear into our hearts."

The Crows or Demons

On April 14, Don Bosco gave the "Good Night" address to the students and on the following night to the artisans. To each group he narrated two dreams which he said had astounded him. The first dream came before the retreat, the second after.

He spoke as follows:

On the night of Saturday, April 2, Low Sunday eve, I seemed to be standing on the balcony watching you at play. Suddenly, a vast white sheet hovered over the entire playground. Then came an enormous flock of crows which fluttered about over the sheet until they found an opening at its edges, dove under it, and flew into the boys' faces, plucking their eyes, ripping their tongues and pecking at their foreheads and hearts! What a pitiful sight! Incredibly, though—I could not believe it— nobody cried or wailed. Everyone seemed to be numb and no one even bothered to defend himself. *"Am I dreaming?"* I wondered, *"I must be. How else could these boys let themselves be butchered like this, without even a whimper?"* Soon, though, I heard a chorus of cries and screams, wailing and whimpering, as the wounded began to crawl away from the others. I did not know what to make of all this. *"Perhaps,"* I thought, *"since it is Low Sunday, the Lord wants to show us that He will shield us with His grace. These crows may be demons."* My musing was suddenly broken off as some noise woke me up. It was daylight, and someone was knocking at my door.

I was surprised on Monday when not as many as usual went to Communion. There were less Communions on Tuesday and very few on Wednesday when, halfway through the Mass, Confessions were over. I decided to say nothing, though, because I hoped that, with the spiritual retreat about to start, matters would be put right.

Last night, April 14, I had another dream. I had been hearing Confessions through the day, and so, as usual, I kept thinking of your spiritual welfare. I went to bed but could not sleep and just dozed for a few hours. Finally, when I did fall asleep, I seemed once again to be standing on the balcony watching you at play. I could spot those who had been hurt by the crows. Suddenly, two personages appeared: one was holding a small jar of ointment, the other a wiping cloth. They immediately began caring for the wounded. As soon as the ointment touched the wounds, the boys were instantly cured. Several, though, refused to be treated and crawled farther back as the two personages got closer to them. What displeased me most was that there were quite a few of these boys. I made a point to jot their names down, because I knew them all, but, as I was writing, I woke up. Since in my dream I had been writing their names, they were still clear in my mind. As a matter of fact, they are clear now, though I may possibly have forgotten some—very few, I am sure. Gradually, I shall speak with those boys—as I have already done with some—and shall try to persuade them to have their wounds treated.

Make what you wish of this dream. I am sure that no spiritual harm will come to you if you believe it fully. But please do not let it out of the Oratory. I am quite open with you, but I want you to keep these things to yourselves.

DON BOSCO'S BELOVED PUPIL ST. DOMINIC SAVIO   **15**

Dominic was born at Riva di Chieri in 1842. When yet a child of seven he received Jesus in his heart for the first time, and in the ardor of his angelic love he then made the following resolutions:

1. My friends shall henceforth be Jesus and Mary.
2. Death rather than sin.

At school he shone forth as a wonderful example of virtue and of application, and at the end of the senior elementary course he left his father's house in order to follow the call from on high.

Dominic's First Meeting with Don Bosco

The scene of that meeting is touching indeed. Don Bosco himself has handed it down to us in the life of the angelic youth. He immediately discovered that Dominic's soul was entirely given up to God and exclaimed: *"Here is good material to form a saint."*

From that day the boy put all his trust and confidence in Don Bosco, who in turn fashioned him into a new St. Aloysius. Dominic had resolved to become a saint. His constant prayer to Don Bosco was: "Father, help me to become a saint." He often manifested the longing of his soul to help others in doing good with the following words: "Oh, would that I could gain all my friends and companions to God! How happy I would then be." Nor was he satisfied with words only, for his prayers, his conversation, his study and even his games were a shining example, a living school of the divine apostolate. His counsels, admonitions, prayers and above all, his sufferings were directed to the sole end of keeping his companions away from evil and of drawing them ever nearer to God. Often he was rapt in ecstasy during Holy Communion. He consecrated his heart to Mary Immaculate.

Dominic's Happy Death

So bright a flower, so tasteful a fruit of divine grace could not remain long on earth. It was soon ripe for Heaven. Thus the brilliant hopes centered in him were doomed to disappointment, for the end of his exile was near and the dawn of eternal light was fast approaching for him.

He knew that his days were numbered, and he looked forward to death with a smiling face. When, on March 9, 1857, in Mondonio d'Asti, the clock of Providence struck his hour, he passed away, exclaiming happily: *"Oh, what a beautiful sight!"* He was then 15 years old.

His mortal remains lie in the Basilica of Mary, Help of Christians in Turin.

After Dominic's death, Don Bosco wrote an account of his life, and it pleased God to glorify the youth by miracles and special favors granted through his intercession.

He was canonized in the year 1954.

The reader is warmly exhorted to read and re-read one of the many lives of St. Dominic Savio. For instance, 1) *Life of St. Dominic Savio* by St. John Bosco, with notes by Fr. Aronica, published by Salesiana Publishers; 2) *The Challenge* by Daniel Higgins (a character study of St. Dominic Savio), published by Salesiana Publishers; 3) *Life of St. Dominic Savio*, SIGA, Madras 600 010; 4) *Dominic Savio, Teenage Saint*, by Peter Lappin, published by the Bruce Publishing Company.

A DREAM ABOUT ST. DOMINIC SAVIO **16**

John Bosco had this dream in 1876, twenty years after Dominic Savio's death.
(*Biographical Memoirs*, Vol. XII, page 586)

On the night of December 6, I dreamed as follows:

It seemed to me that I was standing on a hill, looking down on an immense plain that stretched away into the invisible distance. It was as blue as the sea in perfect calm, but what I was looking at was not water; it seemed like crystal, unblemished and sparkling.

Long and broad avenues divided the plain up into large gardens of indescribable beauty, in which were lawns, groves of ornamental trees, flowering shrubs and flower-beds with an amazing variety of ornamental flowers. What you have seen in gardens can give you little idea of how wonderful all this was. There were trees whose leaves seemed to be of gold, the branches and trunks of precious stones.

Scattered here and there in the gardens were buildings whose appearance and magnificence rivaled the setting in which they stood. I could not estimate what immense sums of money even one of these would have cost to build. The thought ran through my head: "If I could have any one of these buildings for my boys, how happy they would be."

As I stood there rapt in wonder, the sound of sweet and entrancing music filled the air; all possible instruments seemed to be combining in wonderful harmony, and together with them choirs of singers.

I then saw great numbers of people in the garden, some

walking, some sitting, all radiantly happy. Some were singing, some playing instruments, and it was obvious that they derived equal pleasure from hearing the others as they did from the music they were making themselves. They were singing in Latin these words: "All honor and glory to God the Almighty Father—Creator of the ages, who was, who is and who will come to judge the living and the dead through all ages."

There now suddenly appeared a great army of boys. Many of them I knew, boys who had been with me at the Oratory or in one of our schools; but the majority I did not know. This endless line began moving towards me; at its head was Dominic Savio; after him several priests and many other priests and brothers, each at the head of a group of boys.

I did not know whether I was awake or dreaming; I clapped my hands together and felt my arms and chest in the endeavor to see how real was what I was seeing.

An intense, brilliant light now shone all around. All the boys were radiant with happiness; it shone from their eyes, and their faces had a look of ineffable peace and contentment. They smiled at me, and they looked as though they were going to say something, but no word was uttered.

Dominic now walked forward on his own until he stood close beside me. He stood there silently for a moment, smiling and looking at me. How wonderful he looked, how exquisitely he was clothed! The white tunic which reached to his feet was interwoven with golden threads and sparkling jewels. Around his waist he had a broad red sash, also interwoven with precious stones of every color, which sparkled and glittered in a thousand lights. Around his neck there was a necklace of wild flowers, but the flowers were made of precious stones and the light they reflected lit up further still the beauty and dignity of Dominic's face. His hair, which was crowned with roses, hung down to his shoulders and completed the quite indescribable effect of his total appearance.

The others were dressed in varying degrees of splendor, all of which had their own symbolic meaning you would not

St. John Bosco's dream wherein he meets St. Dominic Savio in heavenly glory.

understand. One thing they all had in common was the broad red sash round their waists.

I thought to myself: *"What does all this mean?—Where on earth am I?"* And I stood there silently, not daring to say a word.

Dominic then spoke:

"Why are you standing there as though you were dumb? Are you not the one I knew who was always so fearless, able to sustain persecutions, calumnies and dangers of every kind? Have you lost your courage? Why do you not speak?"

Half stammering, I replied:

"I don't know what to say. Are you really Dominic Savio?"

"Yes, indeed. Don't you recognize me?"

"How is it that you are here?"

"I have come to talk with you," Dominic replied affectionately. "We spoke together so often when I was alive; you were always so kind and generous to me, and I responded to your love with my complete confidence and affection. Ask me anything you wish."

"Where am I?" I asked.

"You are in a place of happiness," he replied, "where all that is beautiful can be enjoyed."

"Is this Heaven, then?"

"No, whatever is here is of the earth, although improved beyond conception by the power of God. No living person can ever see or imagine the wonders of eternity."

"Would it be possible to have natural light more brilliant than this?"

"Yes, quite possible . . . look there in the distance."

I looked, and a ray of light suddenly appeared, so penetrating and of such brilliance that I had to close my eyes, and I cried out in alarm so loudly that I woke the priest who was sleeping in the room nearby. I opened my eyes after a moment and said:

"But that is surely a ray of the divine light . . ."

"No, even that does not give you any idea. In Heaven we enjoy God, and that in everything."

I had by now recovered from my initial amazement and was looking at Dominic as he stood before me. I said:

"Why are you wearing that dazzling white tunic?"

Dominic did not answer, but the choirs of voices beautifully sustained by the many instruments sang in Latin:

"*They had their loins girt and have washed their tunics in the blood of the Lamb.*"

"What does the red sash you wear mean?" I then asked.

Again Dominic did not reply, and a solo voice sang the words:

"*They are virgins and they follow the Lamb wherever He goes.*"

I then realized that the blood-red sash was a symbol of the great efforts and sacrifices made, the quasi-martyrdom suffered, to live a completely pure life. It symbolized also the spirit of penance, which cleanses the soul of its faults. The dazzling white of the tunic represented a life from Baptism to death without any serious rejection of God.

My eyes were drawn to the serried ranks of boys behind Dominic and I asked him:

"Who are these boys, and why are they all so radiant and resplendent?"

The answer came from the boys themselves, who began to sing in wonderful harmony:

"*These are like the angels of God in Heaven . . .*"

Dominic, although the youngest, was obviously the leader, standing out well ahead of them. I therefore asked him:

"Why is that you take precedence over the others?"

"I am the oldest."

"But you are not," I replied; "there are many here much older than you."

"I am God's ambassador."

The meaning of what it was all about suddenly dawned on me, and I hastened to say:

"Let us talk about what concerns me and my work. Perhaps you have something important to tell me . . . Speak to me of the past, present and future of our work and of my dear sons . . ."

"With regard to the past, your Congregation has clearly done much good. Look over there at the great gathering of boys."

I looked and said to him:

"How many they are, and how happy!"

"Look at what is written over the entrance to that garden," said Dominic. I looked and saw written:

Salesian Garden

"All those there are Salesians, or those who have been educated by you and your sons, or who in some way or other have been sent on the way to God and their salvation made really possible. Count them if you can! But they would be many, many more still, if only you had greater faith and confidence in God . . ."

I heaved a great sigh on hearing this admonition and determined to set no limit to my trust in God for the future.

Dominic then held before me a magnificent bunch of flowers; they were roses, violets, sunflowers, lilies, sprigs of evergreen and, most unusual for a bouquet, ears of wheat. He offered it to me and said:

"Look."

"I am looking," I replied, "but I don't understand a thing."

"Make sure that all your boys have it and that they defend it fearlessly against anyone who would try to take it from them. With these flowers secure in their possession, they can never fail to be happy."

"I still don't understand; please explain . . ."

"These flowers represent the virtues and qualities which your boys need in order to be able to live for God instead of for themselves. The rose is the symbol of love, the violet of humility, the sunflower of obedience, the gentian of penance and self-discipline, the ears of corn of frequent Communion, the lily of purity, the sprigs of evergreen of constancy and perseverance."

"No one was adorned with these flowers better than your-self," I said to him. "Tell me what was your greatest conso-lation when you came to die."

"What do you think?" he answered.

I had several attempts at trying to say what I thought it might be, such as having lived such a pure life, having heaped up so much treasure in Heaven by all his good works, and so on, but to all he shook his head with a smile.

"Tell me, then," I said, quite crestfallen at my failure; "what was it?"

"What helped me most and gave me greatest joy when I was dying," replied Dominic, "*was the loving care and help of the great Mother of God.* Tell your sons not to fail to keep close to her while they are alive. But hurry—the time is almost up."

"What about the future?" I asked.

"In this coming year you will have great sorrows to bear. All together, eight of your sons will die. But be of good heart—they will leave this life for Heaven. God is always with you and will give you other sons equally worthy."

"What about the Salesian Congregation?"

"God has great things in store for it. This coming year something will begin which will stretch out to the whole world, from north to south, from east to west. This is only one of many great developments of the future. However, this can only be so on condition that your sons keep to God's way and plan, and not their own.[1]

"*If your priests can be faithful to the mission and way of life God has shown you, the future of the Salesian Congre-gation will be an extraordinary one, and there will be no counting the number of those brought to God through it. There is one further very important condition, however, and that is that you all remain ever close to the great Mother of God*

---

1. The reference is most likely to the Salesian Bulletin, which began in 1877. It has spread right across the world. It is the organ of formation and information for the third Salesian family, the Salesian Co-opera-tors, and has made its own very valuable contribution to Christian fam-ily life in many countries of the world.

and ever proclaim fearlessly by your example the dignity of a pure and chaste life, which is so pleasing to God."

"What about the Church in general?" I then asked.

"What is in store for the Church God alone knows. These are things He reserves to Himself, and they cannot be communicated beforehand to any created being."

"And Pius IX?" I asked.

"This much I can say. He will not have to endure on earth much longer. God will reward him for his faithful service. The Church will not be submerged by present difficulties."

"What about myself?" I asked.

"You have many sorrows and difficulties ahead of you yet . . . but hurry, as my time is almost up."

I stretched out my hands to detain him if I could, but they grasped only the air. Dominic smiled and said:

"What are you trying to do?"

"I don't want to let you go," I said, "but are you bodily here? Are you really my son Dominic?"

"This is how things are. If in God's providence someone who is dead has to appear to someone still alive, he is seen in his normal bodily appearance and distinguishing characteristics. He cannot, however, be bodily touched, since he is a pure spirit. He retains this bodily appearance until he is reunited with his body at the Resurrection."

"One last thing," I now said. "Are all my boys living as children of God? Tell me something that will make it possible for me to help them more."

"You can divide your boys into three groups," Dominic replied, "and these three sheets of paper indicate how."

He handed me the first one. On it was written in large characters:

Unconquered

This sheet contained the names of those who had never been overcome by evil. They were very numerous. I saw them all before me. Many of them I knew; many I saw for the first time. I saw how they lived their lives for God fearlessly and unflinchingly, in spite of the enormous difficulties and dangers they encountered. It was as though they were traveling along a road and were being continually ambushed; they were greatly hindered and molested by the barrage, but never brought down or wounded.

Dominic then gave me the second sheet, on which was written in large characters:

Casualties

On this sheet were the names of those who had seriously offended God, been badly wounded on the journey, but had regained their balance and healed their wounds with a good Confession and Communion, and were trying to press on again, although some showed signs of being discouraged by their experience. They were more in number than on the first sheet. I saw them all and once again recognized many of them.

I held out my hand for the third sheet on which I could see written the words:

Overcome by evil

On the sheet were the names of those who had rejected God by serious sins and were continuing to do so, content to remain deprived of His friendship. I was very anxious to know who they might be and attempted to take the sheet from Dominic.

"Wait a moment," he said to me earnestly. "When you open this sheet, a terrible stench will be given off, which neither you nor I could possibly bear. It is likewise intolerable to the Angels of God, and God Himself."

"How can this be," I said, "the Angels and God being pure spirits?"

"It means this," he replied, "that just as you seek to put the greatest distance possible between yourself and what nauseates you, so those who reject God by serious sin are separated from Him more and more."

He then gave me the sheet, saying:

"Look at it and try to make good use of it for your sons. Never forget the bunch of flowers and try hard to make sure that all have one and never let it go." So saying, he receded from me into the others who were grouped behind him.

I unfolded the sheet . . . I did not see any names, but in a flash I saw before me all those whose names were written. I looked at them with a heavy heart. The majority of them I knew; they belonged to the Oratory or other of our schools. Many of them were normally regarded as good boys and some even as being among the best . . . such they were far from being!

When the paper was unfolded, there arose from it such a horrible stench that I was completely overcome. My head throbbed agonizingly, and I began to vomit so violently that I thought I must die.

Everything became dark, and the vision was no more. A piercing flash of lightning tore across the sky, and as its frightening crash of thunder reverberated in my ear, I awoke trembling with fear.

The stench was still present in my room, clinging to the walls and furniture, and remained there for several days. Thus repugnant to God is the very name of those who reject Him and surrender themselves to the horrors of self-indulgence.

Whenever the memory of that stench comes back to me, I am seized anew with pain and nausea, and I can with difficulty prevent myself from vomiting.

I have spoken with some of the boys whose names I saw written on the lists, and I know for certain that what I saw in the dream is only too true.

BOYS' GIFTS FOR THE BLESSED VIRGIN MARY

(*Biographical Memoirs*, Vol. VIII, page 73)

In the year 1865, while the construction of the church of Mary, Help of Christians was going on, Don Bosco was afflicted by great sorrow over the incurable sickness of four of his priests. One of these saintly priests was Fr. Alasonatti, his first collaborator. But our Blessed Mother came to bring some comfort to her devoted servant during her month of May. The May devotions were celebrated very fervently by one and all at the Oratory.

Of Don Bosco's discourses to the community during the month, only one has been preserved in the chronicle: that of the 30th, and it is a most precious one. Here is a summary of it:

I dreamed that you boys were heading in procession toward a lofty, richly decorated altar of Our Lady. You were all singing the same hymns to her, but not in the same way: many sang beautifully, others rather poorly, and some totally out of tune. I saw too that some kept silent, strayed from the ranks, yawned or kept disturbing others.

Everyone carried gifts, mostly flowers, to Our Lady. The bouquets differed in kind and size. There were bouquets of roses, carnations, violets and so on. Some boys carried very odd presents, such as pigs' heads, cats, slimy toads, rabbits, lambs and so on. A handsome youth stood by the altar. A close look would show that he had wings. He may have been the Oratory's Guardian Angel. As you boys presented your gifts, he took each and placed it on the altar.

The first one to reach the altar offered gorgeous bouquets, which the Angel silently placed on it. From other bouquets, instead, he had to remove decayed or scentless flowers, such as dahlias, camellias and the like, because Mary is not satisfied with mere looks. Some bouquets even had thorns or nails, which of course were promptly plucked out and thrown away.

When a boy carrying a pig's head came up, the Angel said to him, "How dare you offer this to Our Lady? Don't you know that this animal symbolizes the ugly vice of impurity? Mary Most Pure cannot tolerate such a sin. Step aside. You are not worthy to stand in her presence."

To those who offered cats, the Angel said: "Don't you know better? A cat represents theft, and you dare present it to Mary? Those who take what does not belong to them, those who steal food from the house, tear their clothes out of spite, or waste their parents' money by not studying as they ought, are nothing but thieves!" These too the Angel ordered to withdraw. He was equally indignant with boys offering toads. "Toads symbolize the shameful sin of scandal, and dare you offer them to Our Lady? Step aside. Join the unworthy ones." These boys, too, shamefully withdrew.

Some lads came up with a knife stuck in their hearts, a symbol of sacrilege. "Don't you realize that there is death in your soul?" the Angel asked them. "If it were not for God's mercy, you would be lost forever. For heaven's sake, have that knife removed from your heart."

Eventually, the rest of the boys reached the altar and presented their gifts—lambs, rabbits, fish, grapes and so on. The Angel took them and placed them before Our Lady. Then he lined up in front of the altar all the boys whose gifts had been accepted. I noticed to my regret that those who had been made to step aside were much more numerous than I had thought.

Crowns of Roses

Two other Angels now appeared at each side of the altar, carrying ornate baskets filled with most gorgeous, exceedingly beautiful crowns of roses. They were not earthly roses, but heaven-grown, symbolizing immortality. With these the Guardian Angel crowned all the boys ranged before Our Lady's altar. I noticed among them many whom I had never seen before. Another remarkable thing is this: some of the most beautiful crowns went to boys who were so ugly as to be most repulsive. Obviously, the virtue of holy purity, which they eminently possessed, amply made up for their unattractive appearance. Many of the boys possessed this virtue too, though not to the same degree. Youngsters excelling in obedience, humility or love of God were also crowned according to their deserts.

The Angel then addressed all the boys as follows: "It was Our Lady's wish that you should be crowned today with these beautiful roses. See to it that they may never be taken away from you. Humility, obedience and chastity will safeguard them for you. With these three virtues you will always find favor with Mary and one day receive a crown infinitely more beautiful than that you wear today."

All of you then sang the first stanza of the *Ave Maris Stella*—"Hail Star of the Sea!" Afterwards you turned around and filed away as you had come, singing the hymn *Laudate Maria*—"Praise Mary"—so full-heartedly that I was really amazed. I followed you for awhile; then I went back to take a look at the boys whom the Angel had pushed aside, but they were no longer there.

My dear children, I know who was crowned and who was turned down. The latter I will warn privately, so that they may strive to bring gifts pleasing to Our Lady.

Let us make a few observations:

1. All of you were carrying a variety of flowers, but unfailingly, every bouquet had its share of thorns—some more, some less. After much thinking, I came to the conclusion that these thorns symbolize acts of disobedience, such as keeping money instead of depositing it with Father Prefect, asking leave to go to one place and then going to another, being late to school, eating on the sly, going to other boys' dormitories (although knowing that this is always strictly forbidden), lingering in bed after rising time, neglecting prescribed practices of piety, talking during times of silence, buying books and not submitting them for approval, sending or receiving letters on the sly and buying and selling things among yourselves. This is what the thorns stand for.

"Is it a sin to break the house rules?" many will ask. After seriously considering this question, my answer is a firm, "Yes." I will not say whether it is mortal or venial. Circumstances will determine that, but it certainly is a sin.

Some might counter that the Ten Commandments say nothing about obeying house rules. Well, the Fourth Commandment says: "Honor thy father and thy mother." Do you know what father and mother stand for? Not only parents, but also those who take their place. Besides, does not Holy Scripture say: "Obey your superiors"? (*Heb.* 13:17). If you must obey them, it follows that they have the power to command. This is why we have rules, and these must be obeyed.

2. Some bouquets had nails among the flowers, the nails which crucified Jesus. How could that be? As usual, one starts with little things and goes on to more serious ones . . . He allows himself undue liberties and falls into mortal sin. This is how nails managed to find their way into those bouquets, how they again crucified Jesus, as St. Paul says, ". . . crucifying again . . . the Son of God." (*Heb.* 6:6).

3. Many bouquets contained rotten or scentless flowers, symbols of good works done in the state of mortal sin—and therefore unmeritorious—or from human motives, such as

ambition or solely to please teachers and superiors. That is why the Angel, after scolding those boys for daring to offer such things to Our Lady, sent them back to trim their bouquets. Only after they had done this did the Angel accept them and place them on the altar . . . In returning to the altar, these boys did not follow any order, but went up to the Angel as soon as they had trimmed their bouquets, and then joined those to be crowned.

In this dream I saw both your past and your future. I have already spoken of it to many of you. I shall likewise tell the rest. Meanwhile, my children, see to it that the Blessed Virgin may always receive gifts from you which she will not have to refuse.

INNOCENCE PRESERVED BY PENANCE

18

(Biographical Memoirs, Vol. XVII, App. 22)

Persons and Places

In the month of July, 1884, Don Bosco had a dream which lasted all the night. He seemed to have in front of him an immense and beautiful slope, green with vegetation, all smooth and even. On the lower border, this meadow ended in a low step from which one could enter the path where Don Bosco was standing. It seemed an earthly paradise, brilliantly illuminated by a light purer and brighter than the light of the sun. This slope was all covered with tender fresh grass, decked with a thousand kinds of flowers and shaded by a great many beautiful trees which, interwining their branches, stretched out like so many large festoons. In the middle of the garden, reaching to the edges of it, was stretched out a carpet of magic color, which, though not bright, dazzled the sight; it was several miles wide and looked royally magnificent.

By way of ornament, on the band which ran along the border, there were various inscriptions in letters of gold. On one side it read: *Beati immaculati in via, qui ambulant in lege Domini*—"Blessed are they who pass through life's journey unstained, who follow the law of the Lord." On the other side it read: *Non privabit bonis eos qui ambulant in innocentia*—"To innocent lives He will never refuse His bounty." On the third side was written: *Non confundentur in tempore malo; in diebus famis saturabuntur*—"They will not be dismayed by adversity; in time of famine they will be well content." On the fourth side: *Novit Dominus dies immaculatorum, et hereditas eorum in aeternum*—"Jealously the Lord watches over the lives of the guiltless: they will hold their lands forever." On the four corners of the carpet, around a large, magnificent rose, were four other inscriptions: *Cum simplicibus sermocinatio eius*—"His conversation is with the simple." *Proteget gradientes simpliciter*—"He will protect them that walk in simplicity." *Qui ambulant simpliciter ambulant confidenter*—"They that walk sincerely walk confidently." *Voluntas eius in iis qui simpliciter ambulant*—"He will be in them that walk sincerely." Then in the middle of the carpet was written this last one: *Qui ambulat simpliciter salvus erit*—"He that walketh sincerely shall be saved."

In the middle of the slope, on the higher side of the brilliant carpet, there stood a shining banner on which was written in letters of gold: *Fili, tu semper mecum es, omnia mea tua sunt*—"Son, thou art always with me, and all I have is thine."

If Don Bosco had marvelled at the sight of this garden, his attention was even more attracted by two beautiful maidens about twelve years of age who were sitting on the edge of the carpet where the slope ended in a step. The whole of their gracious behavior breathed a heavenly modesty. In their eyes, ever turned upwards, there was not only an ingenuous dove-like simplicity, but there shone forth an ardor of the purest love and a joy of heavenly bliss. Their foreheads, open and serene, seemed to be the seat of candor and sincerity; on their lips played a sweet and charming smile. Their features revealed tender and loving hearts. The graceful movement of their person gave them an air of sovereign dignity and nobility, which contrasted with their youth.

A pure white robe reached to their feet, and on it neither stain nor crease was to be seen, nor the slightest speck of dust. They were girt about with a bright red sash, fringed with gold. On this sash there shone out a garland of flowers composed of lilies, violets and roses. As a necklace they wore a similar garland, composed of the same flowers, but of a different shape. On their wrists they wore bracelets of white daisies.

All these things and flowers had a shape, color and beauty impossible to describe. All the most precious stones in the world, though cut with the most exquisite skill, would seem but mud in comparison. Their white shoes were embroidered with white ribbon interwoven with gold and making a beautiful bow in the center. White, with little threads of gold, were also the laces with which they were tied.

Their long hair was fastened by a crown, which encircled their foreheads, and it was so thick that it curled wave-like from under the crown and fell down on their shoulders.

Praises of Purity

They had begun a dialogue: Now they would speak by turns; now they would ask each other questions and would utter exclamations. Now they would both be sitting down; now one would remain seated while the other would stand, and sometimes they would walk to and fro. But they never went outside that shining carpet, and touched neither the grass nor the flowers.

In his dream Don Bosco was a spectator. He did not say a word to those maidens, nor did they notice his presence. One said to the other in a very sweet voice:—*"What is innocence?"* "The happy state of sanctifying grace preserved by means of the constant and exact observance of the divine law. And the preserved purity of innocence is the fountain and source of all knowledge and virtue."

The first: "What a brilliance, what a glory, what splendor of virtue to live among the wicked and yet to preserve the purity of innocence and the integrity of morals!" The second rose to her feet and, stopping near her companion, exclaimed: "Happy is that youth who does not listen to the counsels of the wicked and does not tread the way of sinners, but whose delight is the law of God, on which he meditates day and night. He shall be as the tree planted near the running waters of God's grace, which will give in its time copious fruit of good works; in spite of the blowing of the winds, the leaves of good intentions and of merits shall not fall from him, and all that he does shall have good results. Every circumstance of his life co-operates in increasing his reward."

So saying, she pointed to the tree of the garden loaded with beautiful fruits, which spread a delicious perfume on the air, while crystal-clear brooklets were flowing now between two flower-covered banks, now falling in little cascades, and now forming small pools, washing around the trunks of the trees, with a murmur like the mysterious sound of far-off music.

The first maiden replied: "He is like a lily among thorns, which the Lord culls in his garden to make it an ornament over His heart, and he can say to his Lord, 'My beloved to me and I to Him, for He feeds among lilies.'" So saying, she pointed to a great number of beautiful lilies, which raised their snow-white cups among the grass and the other flowers, while, in the distance, a very high green hedge surrounded the whole garden. This hedge was made of close-set thorns, and behind it one could see loathsome monsters wandering about like ghosts, trying to get into the garden, but they were prevented by the thorns of the hedge.

"That is right! What truth there is in your words!" added the second. "Happy the youth who will be found without faults! Who is he and we will praise him? For he has done great things in his life; he has been tried and found perfect, and he shall have glory everlasting. He could have sinned, and he did not sin; he could do evil things and has not done them. Therefore are his goods established in the Lord, and all the Church of the Saints shall declare his good works." "And what glory God has set apart for them on earth! He will call them: He will give them a place in His Sanctuary as Ministers of His Mysteries, and He will give them an eternal name, which will never perish," concluded the first.

The second rose to her feet and exclaimed: "Who can

describe the beauty of an innocent soul? Such a soul is splendidly robed like one of us, adorned with the white stole of Baptism. His neck and arms are resplendent with divine jewels; he has on his finger the ring of union with God. He walks lightly on his way to eternity; moreover, there stretches out before him a road adorned with stars . . .

"A living tabernacle of the Holy Ghost, with the Blood of Jesus in his veins, coloring his cheeks and his lips; with the most Holy Trinity in his unspotted heart, he sheds around torrents of light, which clothe him with the brilliance of the sun; a shower of flowers rains down from on high and fills the air. Wafted all round are sweet strains of music of Angels, echoing his prayer. Mary Most Holy stands beside him, ready to defend him. Heaven is open to him. He is a charming sight to the immense legion of Saints and blessed spirits, who receive and welcome him. God, in the unapproachable splendor of His glory, points out with His right hand the throne He has prepared for him, while in His left hand He holds the shining crown which is to adorn him forever.

"The innocent is the desire, the joy, the applause of Paradise. His face is adorned with ineffable joy. He is God's son; he has God for a father and Paradise for his inheritance. He is continually with God: he sees Him, loves Him; he possesses and enjoys Him; he has a ray of the delights of Heaven: he is in possession of all His gifts and of His perfections."

"That is why innocence in the Saints of the Old Testament, in the Saints of the New Testament and especially in the Martyrs appears so glorious!

"O Innocence, how beautiful you are! When tempted, you increase in perfection; when humbled you rise more sublime; in the combat you come forth victorious; and in death you fly to your crown. In slavery you are free; in dangers you are tranquil and safe; in chains you are happy. The powerful bow down to you; the rulers welcome you; and the great seek you. The good obey you; the wicked envy you; your rivals emulate you; your adversaries succumb to you. Should men unjustly condemn you, you will always come out victorious."

The Delicacy of Chastity
The Misfortunes of Him Who Loses It

The two maidens paused an instant, as if to regain breath after such an ardent exertion, and then they took hold of each other by the hand and, looking at each other, continued:

"Oh, if the young knew what precious treasure innocence is, how jealously they would guard the stole of Holy Baptism right from the beginning of their life! But unfortunately they do not reflect, and they do not imagine what it means to stain it!"

"Innocence is a most precious liquor, but it is enclosed in a vessel of frail clay."

"Innocence is a very precious gem, but its value is not known; it is lost and easily exchanged for a worthless object."

"Innocence is a golden mirror which reflects the image of God. But a breath of damp air is enough to dim it, and one must keep it covered with a veil."

"Innocence is a lily."

"But the mere touch of a rough hand spoils it."

"Innocence is a white robe: *Omni tempore sint vestimenta tua candida*—'Let your garments be glittering white at all times.' "

"But one single stain is enough to soil it; therefore, one must walk with great precaution."

"Innocence is integrity; it is lost if it is spoiled by a single sin, and it loses the treasure of its beauty."

"Just one mortal sin is sufficient, and once it is lost, it is lost forever."

"What a pity that every day so many lose their innocence! When a boy falls into sin, Paradise is closed; the Most Holy Virgin and his Angel Guardian disappear; the music ceases; the light is put out; God is no longer in his heart; the starry road which he had trodden vanishes; he falls and remains on one point like an island in the middle of the sea, a sea of fire, which extends to the furthermost horizon of eternity and goes down to the depths of chaos. Above his head, in the darkened sky, the lightning of the Divine Justice flashes threateningly. Satan has rushed upon him and loaded him with chains, has placed his foot upon his neck, and raising his horribly ugly snout, has cried out: 'I have conquered! Your son is my slave; he belongs to you no more!' Joy is over for him. If, at that moment, the justice of God takes away that one point which supports him, he is lost forever."

"He can rise again! God's mercy is infinite. A good Confession will give back the grace of God and the title of son of God."

"But no more innocence! And what consequences of the first sin will remain in him! He knows evil, which he did not know before; he will feel how terrible are his base inclinations; he will feel the enormous debt which he has contracted with the Divine Justice; in spiritual combats he will be weaker. He will experience what he never experienced before; namely, shame, sadness and remorse."

"And to think that before it was said of him: 'Suffer little children to come unto me. They will be as the Angels of God in Heaven' . . . 'Son, give me thy heart . . .' "

"Woe to Those Who Give Scandal!"

"Oh, what a frightful crime is committed by those wretches through whose fault a child loses its innocence! Jesus has said: 'He that shall scandalize one of these little ones that believe in me, it were better for him that a millstone should be hanged about his neck and that he should be drowned in the depths of the sea.' 'Woe to the world because of scandals!' 'It is not possible to avoid scandals; but woe to him through whose fault the scandal comes . . .' 'See that you despise not any of these little ones, for I say to you that *their Angels* in Heaven always see the face of My Father, who is in Heaven, and they demand vengeance.' "

"Unfortunate is the scandal-giver, but not less unhappy are those who allow themselves to be robbed of their innocence!"

Means for Preserving Innocence

Here both maidens began to walk about. The subject of their conversation was concerning the best means for preserving innocence. One of them said:

"A great mistake which boys make is that of thinking that penance must be practiced by sinners only. Penance is necessary also in order to preserve innocence. If St. Aloysius had not done penance, he would certainly have fallen into mortal sin. This should be continually preached, inculcated and taught to children. How many more would preserve their innocence, while at present there are so few!"

"The Apostle says that we must carry everywhere with us the mortification of Jesus Christ in our bodies, that also the life of Jesus may be manifest in us."

"And Jesus, the Holy, the Immaculate One, passed His life in privations and sufferings."

"So did Mary Most Holy; so did all the Saints."

"It was to give an example to all youths. St. Paul says: '*If you live according to the flesh, you shall die; but if according to the spirit, you shall give the death-blow to the inclinations of the flesh, you shall live.*'"

"Therefore, *without penance, innocence cannot be preserved.*"

"And yet many would like to preserve their innocence and live a free and easy life . . ."

"Fools! Is it not written, 'He was taken away, that wickedness might not contaminate his spirit, nor seduction lead his mind into error?' Because the charm of vanity does not bring any good, and the whirlpool of concupiscence drowns the innocent soul. So the innocent have two enemies: 1) the false maxims and the bad conversations of the wicked, and 2) concupiscence. Does not the Lord say that death at an early age is a reward for the innocent, to take him away from the combats? 'Because he pleased God, he was beloved, and because he was living among sinners, he was taken away. Being made perfect in a short space, he fulfilled a long time. For his soul pleased God; therefore He hastened to bring him out of the midst of iniquities. He was taken away lest wickedness should alter his understanding or deceit beguile his soul.'" (*Wis.* 4:10-14).

"*Happy those children who will embrace the cross of penance* and with a firm resolution will say with Job: *Donec deficiam, non recedam ab innocentia mea*—'Till I die, I will not depart from my innocence.'"

"*Hence mortification in overcoming weariness in prayer.* It is written: *Psallam et intelligam in via immaculata;* . . . *quando venies ad me?* . . . *Petite et accipietis. Pater Noster!*—'I will sing and I will understand in the unspotted way. When shalt thou come? Ask and you shall receive. Our Father!'"

"*Mortification of the intellect by humbling oneself*: Obeying the Superiors and the rules.

"It is also written: *Si mei non fuerint dominati tunc immaculatus ero et emundabor a delicto maximo*—'If they shall have no dominion over me, then shall I be without spot.' (*Ps.* 18:14). And this sinful dominion is pride. 'God resisteth the proud and giveth His grace to the humble'; 'He that humbles himself shall be exalted, and he that exalteth himself shall be humbled!'"

"*Obey your Superiors.*"

"*Mortifications in telling the truth always*, in revealing one's defects and the dangers in which one may find oneself. Then one will always have suitable advice, especially from one's confessor. *Pro anima tua non confundaris dicere verum*—'For the love of your soul do not be ashamed to tell the truth.' For there is a blush which brings sin with it, and there is a blush which brings glory and grace."

"*Mortifications of the heart, checking its thoughtless movements*, loving all for God's love, tearing oneself resolutely from anyone we perceive to be endangering our innocence. Jesus said: 'If thy hand and foot scandalize thee, cut them off and cast them from thee. It is better for thee to enter into life having one foot or one hand missing, than with both hands and both feet to be cast into everlasting fire.'"

"Mortification in supporting courageously and frankly the

mockery of human respect: *Exacuerunt ut gladium linguas suas; intenderunt arcum, rem amaram, ut sagittent in occultum immaculatum*—'They have whetted their tongues like a sword; they have bent their bow, a bitter thing, to shoot in secret the undefiled.' "

"This human respect, which mocks while fearing to be discovered by the Superiors, will be conquered by thinking of the terrible words of Jesus Christ: '*He who is ashamed of Me and My words, the Son of Man will be ashamed of him, when He shall come in His majesty . . .*' "

"*Mortification of the eyes, in looks, in reading, shunning bad and unsuitable literature.*"

"An essential point: 'I have made a contract with my eyes never to look at a maiden.' And in the *Psalms*: 'Turn away thine eyes that they see not vanity.' "

"*Mortification of the hearing, never listening to bad, imprudent or impious conversations.* In *Ecclesiasticus* we read: *Sepi aures tuas spinis, linguam nequam noli audire*—'Put a hedge of thorns around thine ears and do not listen to the wicked tongue.' "

"*Mortification in speech*, not allowing oneself to be overcome by curiosity."

"It is also written: 'Put a door and bolt to your mouth. Take care not to sin with the tongue, so that you may not fall to the ground at the sight of the enemies who oppose you and that your fall be not incurable and mortal.' "

"*Mortification in eating and drinking*, neither eating nor drinking too much. Too much eating and drinking drew down the universal flood upon the earth, and fire on Sodom and Gomorrha, and a thousand chastisements on the Hebrews."

"*In short, to mortify oneself in all that happens throughout the day*: cold and heat, and never seeking our personal satisfaction: 'Mortify your earthly limbs.' Remember what Jesus has commanded: '*Si quis vult post me venire, abneget semetipsum, tollat crucem suam, et sequatur me*'—'If any man will come after Me, let him deny himself and take up his cross, and follow Me.' "

Holy Communion
Devotion to Mary

"God Himself, with His provident hand, girds His innocents with crosses and thorns, as He did with Job, Joseph, Tobias and other Saints. *Quia acceptus eras Deo, neccesse fuit ut tentatio probaret te*—'Because thou wast acceptable to God, it was necessary that temptation should try thee.'"

"The way of the innocent has its trials and sacrifices, but it has its strength in Holy Communion, because he who communicates frequently has eternal life: he is in Jesus, and Jesus is in him. He who lives of the same life as Jesus will be raised up by Him at the last day. This is the wheat of the elect, and the wine which produces virgins. *Parasti in conspectu tuo mensam adversus eos qui tribulant me. Cadent a latere tuo mille, et decem milia a dexteris tuis: ad te autem non appropinquabunt*—'Thou hast prepared a table before thee, against them that afflict me. A thousand shall fall at thy side, and ten thousand at thy right hand, but they will not come nigh to thee.'"

"And the Virgin most sweet, beloved by him, is a Mother to him. *Ego mater pulchrae dilectionis et timoris et agnitionis et sanctae spei. In me gratia omnis viae et veritatis; in me omnis spes vitae et virtutis. Ego diligentes me diligo. Qui elucidant me vitam aeternam habebunt. Terribilis ut castrorum acies ordinata*—'I am the mother of fair love and of fear and of knowledge, and of holy hope. In me is all the grace of the way and of the truth, in me is all hope of life and of virtue. I love them that love me. They that shall explain me shall have life everlasting. Terrible as an army set in array.'"

The two maidens then turned around and went slowly up the slope; and one of them exclaimed:

"The safety of the just comes from the Lord, and He is their protector in the time of tribulation. The Lord will help them and set them free; He will take them out of the hand of sinners and will save them, because they have hoped in Him."

"God girded me with strength," continued the other, "and made spotless the path which I tread."

When the two maidens reached the middle of the magnificent carpet, they turned around.

"Yes," cried one, "*innocence crowned with penance is the queen of virtues.*" And the other exclaimed:

"How glorious and beautiful is the chaste generation! Its memory is immortal and known both to God and men. People imitate it when it is present, and wish for it when it has departed for Heaven, triumphantly crowned in eternity, having won the reward of its chaste combats.

"And what a triumph, what a joy to present immaculate to God the stole of Holy Baptism, after so many combats, amidst the applauses, the hymns and the splendor of the heavenly hosts!"

While they were thus speaking of the reward which is prepared for "innocence preserved by penance," Don Bosco saw bands of Angels appear, descending on the shining white carpet and joining the two maidens, who always remained in the center. They were a great multitude, and they sang:

Benedictus Deus et Pater Domini Nostri Jesu Christi QUI BENEDICIT NOS . . . in ipso ante mundi constitutionem ut essemus sancti et immaculati in conspectu ejus in caritate, qui praedestinavit nos in adoptionem filiorum per Jesum Christum—"Blessed be God and the Father of Our Lord Jesus Christ, who hath blessed us . . . in Him before the foundation of the world, that we should be holy and unspotted in His sight in charity, who hath predestinated us unto the adoption of children through Jesus Christ."

The Canticle of Innocence

The two maidens then began to sing an amazing hymn, with such words and notes as only those Angels who were nearest to the center could make. The others also sang, but Don Bosco could not hear their voices, although they were making gestures and moving their lips and shaping their mouths as if singing. The maidens sang:

Me propter innocentiam suscepisti et confirmasti me in conspectu tuo in aeternum. Benedictus Deus a saeculo. Fiat! Fiat! —"Thou hast upheld me by reason of my innocence and hast established me in Thy sight forever. Blessed be God from eternity to eternity. So be it! So be it!"

Meanwhile, the first band of Angels was being joined by others in ever-increasing numbers; their dress had a charming variety of colors and ornaments, each one different from the others, especially from those of the maidens. But the richness and magnificence was divine. The beauty of each one of them was such that no human mind can imagine even the shadow of it; the whole spectacle of this scene cannot be described; but by adding words to words, it is possible in some way to give at least an imperfect idea of it.

When the maidens had stopped singing, the whole company was heard to raise together an immense canticle, so harmonious that its equal was never heard on earth, nor will ever be heard. They sang:

Ei qui potest vos conservare sine peccato et constituere ante conspectum gloriae suae immaculatos in exultatione, in adventu Domini Nostri Jesu Christi: soli Deo Salvatori Nostri per Jesum Christum Dominum nostrum, gloria et magnificentia, imperium et potestas ante omne saeculum et nunc et in omnia saecula saeculorum. Amen.—"To Him who is able to preserve you without sin and to present you spotless before the presence of His glory with exceeding joy in the coming of Our Lord Jesus Christ: to the Only God, Our Saviour, through Jesus Christ Our Lord, be glory and magnificence, empire and power, before all ages, and now, and for all ages. Amen."

While they were singing, more and more Angels were continually joining them, and when the canticle was finished, little by little they all rose on high and disappeared; thus vanished the whole vision.

IN THE LAND OF TRIAL

19

(*Biographical Memoirs*, Vol. XI, page 239ff.)

In his "Good Night" address on April 30, 1875, Don Bosco exhorted the boys to make devoutly the May devotions. After urging them, therefore, to greater diligence in the fulfillment of their duties and the choice of some special act of devotion in honor of Mary, he added that he had a dream to tell them, but since it was already late, he would tell it on the following Sunday.

The boys were beside themselves with impatience. Their curiosity was further aroused by another two-day postponement because Don Bosco was busy. Finally, on the evening of May 4, their curiosity was satisfied. After prayers, Don Bosco addressed them as usual from the little pulpit:

Here I am to keep my promise. You know that dreams come during sleep. As the time for the retreat drew near, I was wondering how my boys would make it and what I should suggest to make it fruitful. On Sunday night, April 25, the eve of the retreat, I went to bed with this thought in my mind. I fell asleep immediately, and I seemed to be standing all alone in a vast valley enclosed on both sides by high hills. At the far end of the valley, along one side where the ground rose steeply, there was a pure, bright light; the other side was in semi-darkness. As I stood gazing at the plain, Buzzetti and Gastini came up to me and said: "Don Bosco, you will have to mount a horse. Hurry! Hurry!"

"Are you joking?" I said, "You know how long it has been since I last rode a horse." They insisted, but in an attempt to excuse myself, I kept repeating, "I don't want to ride a horse; I did it once and fell off."

Gastini and Buzzetti kept pressing me ever more and said: "Get on a horse, and quickly. There is no time to lose."

"But suppose I do mount a horse, where are you taking me?"

"You'll see. Now, hurry and mount."

"But where's the horse? I don't see any."

"There it is," shouted Gastini, pointing to one side of the valley. I looked and saw a beautiful, spirited steed. It had long, strong legs, a thick mane and a very glossy coat.

"Well, since you want me to mount it, I will. But woe to you if I fall . . ." I said.

"Don't worry," they replied, "We'll be here with you for emergency."

"And if I break my neck, you'll have to fix it," I told Buzzetti.

Buzzetti broke into a laugh. "This is not time to laugh," Gastini muttered.

We walked over to the horse. Even with their help, I had great difficulty mounting, but finally I was in the saddle. How tall that horse seemed to be then! It was as if I were perched on top of a high mound from where I could survey the entire valley from end to end.

Then the horse started to move. Strangely, while this was happening, I seemed to be in my own room. I asked myself, "Where are we?" Coming towards me I saw priests, clerics and others; all looked frightened and breathless.

After a long ride, the horse stopped. Then I saw all the priests of the Oratory together with many of the clerics approaching. They gathered around the horse. I recognized Fr. Rua, Fr. Cagliero and Fr. Bologna among them. When they reached me, they stopped and silently stared at my horse. I noticed that all seemed worried. Their disquiet was such as I had never seen before. I beckoned to Fr. Bologna.

"Fr. Bologna," I said, "you are in charge of the main entrance; can you tell me what happened? Why do you look so upset?"

"I don't know where I am or what I am doing," he said. "I'm all confused . . . Some people came in . . . talked and left . . . There is such a hubbub of people coming and going at the main entrance that I don't know what's going on."

"Is it possible," I wondered, "that something very unusual might happen today?"

Just then someone handed me a trumpet, saying I should hold on to it because I would need it.

"Where are we now?" I asked.

"Blow the trumpet!"

I did, and heard these words: "We are in the land of trial."

Pitchforks and Battle

Then I saw a multitude of boys—I think over 100 thousand—coming down the hills. There was absolute silence. Carrying pitchforks, they were hastening towards the valley. I recognized among them all the Oratory boys and those of our other schools; but there were many more unknown to me. Just then on one side of the valley the sky darkened and hordes of animals resembling lions and tigers appeared. These ferocious beasts had big bodies, strong legs and long necks, but their heads were quite small. They were terrifying. With blood-shot eyes bulging from their sockets, they hurled themselves at the boys, who immediately stood ready to defend themselves. As the animals attacked, the boys stood firm and beat them off with their pronged pitchforks, which they lowered or raised as needed.

Unable to overpower them by this first attack, the beasts snapped at the fork prongs, only to break their teeth and vanish. Some of the boys, however, had forks with only one prong, and these were wounded. Others had pitchforks with broken or worm-eaten handles, and still others threw themselves at the beasts bare-handed and fell victims; quite a few of these were killed. Many had pitchforks with two prongs and new handles.

While this was going on, from the very start swarms of serpents slithered about my horse. Kicking and stamping, the horse crushed and drove them off: at the same time it kept growing ever taller and taller.

I asked someone what the two-pronged forks symbolized. I was handed a fork. On the prongs I read: Confession, on one; Communion, on the other.

"But what do the prongs mean?"

"Blow the trumpet!"

I did, and heard these words: "Good Confession and good Communion." I blew the trumpet again and heard these words: "Broken handle: sacrilegious Confessions and Communions. Worm-eaten handle: faulty Confessions."

Dead and Wounded

Now that the first attack was over, I rode over the battle-field and saw many dead and wounded. I saw that some of the dead had been strangled and their necks were swollen and deformed. The faces of others were horribly disfigured; still others had starved to death while enticing food was within their reach. The boys who were strangled are those who unfortunately committed some sins in their early years and never confessed them: those with disfigured faces are gluttons; and the boys who died of hunger are those who go to Confession but never follow the advice or admonition of their confessor.

The Thorns

Next to each boy whose pitchfork had a worm-eaten handle, a word stood out. For some it was *Pride;* for others, *Sloth;* for others still, *Immodesty*, etc. . . . I must also add that in their march the boys had to walk over a bed of roses. They liked it, but after a few steps they would utter a cry and fall to the ground either dead or wounded because of the thorns hidden underneath. Others instead bravely trampled on those roses and, encouraging one another, marched on to victory.

New Battle and Victory

Then the sky darkened again. Instantly, even greater hordes of the same animals or monsters appeared. All this happened in less than three or four seconds. My horse was surrounded. The monsters increased beyond count and I too began to be frightened. I could feel them clawing at me! Then someone handed me a pitchfork, and I also began to fight them, and the monsters were forced to retreat. Beaten in their first attack, they all vanished.

Then I blew the trumpet again, and these words echoed through the valley: "*Victory! Victory!*"

"Victory?" I wondered, "how is it possible with so many dead and wounded?"

I blew the trumpet once more and we heard the words: "Truce for the vanquished!" The sky brightened and a rainbow became visible. It was so lovely and so colorful that I cannot describe it. It was immense, as though one end rested on top of Superga[1] and its arch stretched and stretched until it reached the top of Moncenisio. I should also add that all the boys who had been victorious wore crowns so brilliant and so bright and varied in color that it was an awe-inspiring sight. Their faces, too, were resplendently handsome. At the far end of the valley was a sort of balcony, holding peo-

---

1. Superga: a hill about three miles east of Turin. From the summit of the hill, 2205 ft. above sea-level, in fine weather one can look down on Turin or at the wide semicircle of the snow crested Alps that rise like a wall at a radius of thirty miles or more. On top of this hill rises a famous basilica. (Cf. *Biographical Memoirs*, Vol. II, p. 298.)

ple full of joy and of such varied beauty as to surpass my imagination.

A very noble lady, royally arrayed, came to the railing of the balcony and called out: *"Come, my children, and take shelter under my mantle."* As she spoke, an immense mantle spread out and all the boys ran to take cover under it. Some actually flew; these had the word *Innocence* on their forehead. Others just walked; and some crawled. I also started to run, and in that split second—it couldn't have been more than that—I said to myself: "This had better end or we'll die." I had just said this and was still running when I woke up.

Explanation

For reasons later explained, Don Bosco returned to this subject on May 6, the Feast of the Ascension. He had the students and the artisans assembled together for night prayers, and then he spoke as follows:

The other night I was not able to say everything because we had visitors in our midst. These things must be kept among us, and no one should write to friends or relatives about them. I confide everything in you, even my sins.

The valley, that land of trial, is this world. The semi-darkness is the place of perdition; the two hills are the Commandments of God and of the Church; the serpents are the devils; the monsters, evil temptations; the horse, I think, is the same as the one that struck Heliodorus[2] and represents our trust in God. The boys who walked over the roses and fell dead are those who give in to this world's pleasures that deal death to the soul; those who trampled the roses underfoot are those who spurn worldly pleasures and are therefore victorious. The boys who flew under the mantle are those who have preserved their baptismal innocence.

---

2. *2 Machabees,* Ch. 3.

For the sake of those who might wish to know, little by little I shall tell those concerned the kind of weapon they carried and whether they were victorious or not, dead or wounded. I did not know all the boys, but I recognized those of the Oratory. And if the others were ever to come here I would recognize them immediately the moment I saw them.

Questions

Fr. Berto, Don Bosco's secretary who took down this dream, wrote that he could not remember many things that Don Bosco had narrated and explained at length. The next morning, May 7, when he was with Don Bosco, he asked him: *"How can you possibly remember all the boys you saw in your dream, and tell each one the state he was in and pinpoint his faults?"* "Oh," Don Bosco answered, "by means of Otis Botis Pia Tutis." This was a meaningless phrase that he often used to evade embarrassing questions.

When Fr. Barberis also broached the same subject, Don Bosco said gravely: *"It was a great deal more than a dream"*; and cutting the talk short, he passed on to other things.

Fr. Berto ends his report with these words: "I, too, the writer of this report, asked him about my part in this dream. His answer was so much to the point that I burst into tears and said, 'An Angel from Heaven could not have hit the truth better.'"

More Questions

Once again this dream was the theme of another "Good Night" address on June 4. The community was present at this dialogue between Fr. Barberis and Don Bosco.

Fr. Barberis: "With your permission, Don Bosco, this evening I would like to ask a few questions. I didn't dare to ask these last few evenings, because we had visitors. I'd like some clarification on your last dream."

Don Bosco: "Go ahead. It is some time since I last mentioned it, but it doesn't matter."

Fr. Barberis: "You said at the end of your dream that some flew to Mary's mantle, some ran, others walked slowly and a few sloshed through mud, were bespattered with it and were hardly able to take cover under the mantle. You already told us that those who flew were the pure. We can easily understand those who ran, but what is meant by those who got stuck in the mud?"

Don Bosco: "Those who got stuck in the mud and who, for the most part, could not reach Our Lady's mantle symbolize those attached to the things of this world. Being selfish, they think only of themselves; and because of this they bespatter themselves with mud and are no longer able to get off the ground and aspire to the things of Heaven. They see the Blessed Virgin calling to them and would like to go to her. They take a few steps, but the mud holds them down. It always happens like that. The Lord says: '*Where thy treasure is, there also will your heart be.*' (*Matt.* 6:21). Those who do not raise themselves up to the treasures of grace set their hearts on the things of this world. Pleasures, riches, success in business, vainglory are all they think of. Heaven is just ignored."

Fr. Barberis: "There is something else you did not tell us about, Don Bosco. You mentioned it to some privately, and I wish you would let us know, too. It is this: Someone asked you whether he was among those who ran or those who walked slowly, and if he had taken cover under the mantle of Mary, and if the handle of his pitchfork was worm-eaten or broken. You replied that you had been unable to see clearly because there was a cloud between you and him."

Don Bosco: "You are a theologian and you should know. Well, there were indeed some boys, though not very many, whom I could not see clearly. I saw each of them well enough to recognize them, but that was about all. *Those are the boys who are tight-lipped with their Superiors; they do not open their hearts to them*; they are not sincere. Whenever they see a Superior coming their way, rather than meet him, they go off in the opposite direction. Some of them came to ask me in what state I had seen them in the dream. But what could I tell them? I could have said: You have no confidence in your Superiors; you never open your heart to them. Now all of you remember this! *There is nothing that can be of greater help to you than opening your hearts to your Superiors, having greater trust in them and being utterly sincere.*"

Fr. Barberis: "There is something else I'd like to ask, but I'm afraid you might say I am too curious."

Don Bosco: "Isn't that fairly well-known? (general laughter). Yet, you know there is a certain kind of curiosity which is healthy, as for example, when a boy anxious to learn keeps asking questions about serious things from persons who might know. There are others instead who just stand around like fools. They never have any questions to ask. This is not a good reflection on them."

Fr. Barberis: "Well, I won't be like that. For a long time I have wanted to ask you this question about the dream. Did you see only each boy's past, or did you also see his future, that is, his vocation and his possible success?"

Don Bosco: "I saw more than the past; I also saw the future that was to be theirs. Each boy had several paths stretching out ahead of him. Some were narrow and thorny; others were strewn with sharp nails, but God's blessing had also been strewn on these paths. All these paths led to a garden of rare beauty filled with every delight."

Fr. Barberis: "Then this means that you can tell which path each one should take, that is, you know the vocation of each one of us, how we shall end up, and which path we shall follow."

Don Bosco: "No. It would not be wise to tell each one which path he will follow or how he will end up. No good will result from telling a boy: 'You will take the path of wickedness.' This would only frighten him. What I can say is this: If one follows a certain path he may be sure that he is on the road to Heaven, on the road, namely, to which he has been called; and, if one does not follow that road, he will not be on the right path. Some roads are narrow, uneven and strewn with thorns; yet, take heart, my dear children, with the thorns there is also the grace of God, and so much happiness is in store for us at the end of our journey that we shall soon forget all our pain. Honestly, I would like all of you to remember this: This was a dream, no one is obliged to believe it. I have noticed, however, that those who have asked me for explanations have accepted my suggestions in good part. Nevertheless, do as St. Paul says: *Probate spiritus et quod bonum est tenete*—'Scrutinize carefully, retain what is good.' (*1 Thess.* 5:21). Another thing that I would want you not to forget is to pray for your poor Don Bosco, lest the words of St. Paul: *Cum aliis praedicaverim, ego reprobus afficiar*—'After preaching to others, I myself should be rejected' (*1 Cor.* 9:27) may apply to me. That is, after preaching to you, I may end up with the damned. I am doing my best to warn you, I worry about you and give you advice, but I fear I may be acting like a brooding hen that hunts for crickets, worms, seeds and other food for her chicks while she herself may die of hunger, unless she gets some good nourishment. Therefore, pray to God for me that this may not happen, but that, instead, I may adorn my heart with many virtues and be pleasing to God, so that one day all of us may go to Heaven to enjoy Him and glorify Him. Good night."

A GHASTLY PIT **20**

(*Biographical Memoirs*, Vol. VII,
pages 333-334)

November 13, 1863, at the "Good Night" address, Don Bosco said:

Yesterday morning we made the Exercise for a happy death. Now I fear that some of you did not make it well. Let me tell you a dream I had last night.

I was with you in the playground while you were all playing. Then we all went for a stroll to a meadow, where you resumed your pastimes, mostly jumping games. Suddenly, I spotted an unguarded pit in the center of the meadow and hastened over to make sure it was safe. As I looked into it, I saw a short, yellow-spotted, mean-looking serpent coiled at the bottom. It seemed as huge as a horse or even as an elephant. I leaped back in fright.

Meanwhile, a good number of you began jumping over the pit. Oddly enough, it never dawned on me to stop you or alert you to the danger. I noticed that while the younger boys were leaping over it nimbly, the older ones, being heavier, often clumsily landed on the very edge. Each time this happened, the serpent would strike out, nip its victim's foot, leg or other part of his body, and quickly drop out of sight. Unconcerned, these foolhardy lads kept jumping, though they hardly ever went unscathed. As this was going on, a boy, pointing to a companion, said, "He'll jump once and barely make it. Then he'll jump again, and that will be the end of him."

Risking

Grieved to see boys lying about wounded in legs, arms and even hearts, I asked: "Why did you jump over the pit and keep it up even after you got hurt?"

"We're still not too good at jumping," they replied with a sigh.

"Then you shouldn't have jumped!"

"We couldn't help it. We're just not too good at it. Besides, we didn't think it was so risky."

One boy in particular really shook me—the lad who had been pointed out to me. On his second leap he failed and fell into the pit. Moments later he was spewed out, black as coal, though still breathing and able to speak. We all stared at him in terror and kept asking him questions.

The Ruffino chronicle says nothing more. It is utterly silent about the dream's interpretation and the admonitions—all the more necessary at the start of a new school year, which Don Bosco undoubtedly gave the boys publicly and privately. What are we to say? Can we offer an explanation?

Explanation

The pit is the one mentioned in Holy Scripture: ". . . a deep ditch," "a narrow pit" (*Prov.* 23:27), "the pit of destruction" (*Ps.* 54:24). *In it lies the demon of impurity,* as St. Jerome tells us in his eleventh homily on St. Paul's first letter to the Corinthians. Seemingly, the dream does not point to souls already enslaved by sin, but to those who place themselves in danger of sin. At this point, light-heartedness, fun and peace of heart begin to fade away. The younger boys jump nimbly and safely over the pit, because their passions are still dormant. Blissfully innocent, they are fully engrossed in their games, and their Guardian Angels safeguard their innocence and simplicity. The dream, though, does not say that they kept jumping over the pit. Perhaps they heeded a friend's advice.

The older boys too want to leap, but they are out of practice and not as nimble as their companions. Furthermore, they have felt the strain of their first battles against the flesh and are not aware of the serpent's ambush. *"Is jumping over that pit really so terribly risky?"* they seem to ask. And then the game begins. Their first leap may begin to materialize when they start forming *emotional friendships, accepting objectionable books and nursing strong attachments.* Being too free and boisterous, they keep away from good companions and disregard rules or admonitions to which superiors attach serious importance in the safeguarding of their morals.

The first jump ends in a serpent's bite. Some boys escape harm and prudently take no more chances. Others, rashly disregarding a real danger, go back to it. It seems that *falling into the pit and being tossed out again symbolized a fall into mortal sin, but with a chance of recovery through the Sacraments.* Of those who fell and remained in the pit nothing more need be said than: *"He who loves danger will perish in it."* (*Ecclus.* 3:27).

N.B. Of great interest to educators is the chapter that follows the above narration, pages 335-340 of Vol. VII.

TEN HILLS 21

(*Biographical Memoirs*, Vol. VII, pages 467-470)

October 1864: Don Bosco seemed to be in a vast valley swarming with thousands and thousands of boys—so many, in fact, that their number surpassed belief. Among them he could see all past and present pupils; the rest, perhaps, were yet to come. Scattered among them were priests and clerics then at the Oratory.

A lofty bank blocked one end of the valley. As Don Bosco wondered what to do with all those boys, a voice said to him: "Do you see that bank? Well, both you and the boys must reach its summit."

At Don Bosco's word, all those youngsters dashed toward the bank. The priests too ran up the slope, pushing the boys ahead, lifting up those who fell, and hoisting on their shoulders those who were too tired to climb farther. Fr. Rua, his sleeves rolled up, kept working hardest of all, gripping two boys at a time and literally hurling them up to the top of the bank, where they landed on their feet and merrily scampered about. Meanwhile, Fr. Cagliero and Fr. Francesia ran back and forth encouraging the youngsters to climb.

It did not take long for all of them to make it to the top. "*Now what shall we do?*" Don Bosco asked.

"You must all climb each of the ten hills before you," the voice replied.

"Impossible! So many young, frail boys will never make it!"

"Those who can't will be carried," the voice countered.

The Innocent

At this very moment, at the far end of the bank, appeared a gorgeous, triangular-shaped wagon, too beautiful for words. Its three wheels swiveled in all directions. Three shafts rose from its corners and joined to support a richly embroidered banner, carrying in large letters the inscription *Innocentia*—"Innocence." A wide band of rich material was draped about the wagon, bearing the legend: *Adiutorio Dei Altissimi, Patris et Filii et Spiritus Sancti*—"With the help of the Most High God, Father, Son and Holy Spirit."

Glittering with gold and gems, the wagon came to a stop in the boys' midst. At a given order, five hundred of the smaller ones climbed into it. Among the untold thousands, only these few hundred were still innocent.

The Penitent

As Don Bosco kept wondering which way to go, a wide, level road strewn with thorns opened before him. Suddenly, there also appeared six white-clad former pupils who had died at the Oratory. Holding aloft another splendid banner with the inscription *Penitentia*—"Penance"—they placed themselves at the head of the multitude, which was to walk the whole way. As the signal to move was given, many priests seized the wagon's prow and led the way, followed by the six white-clad boys and the rest of the multitude. The lads in the wagon began singing *Laudate pueri Dominum*—"Praise the Lord, you children" (*Ps.* 112:1)—with indescribable sweetness.

Don Bosco kept going forward, enthralled by their heavenly melody, but, on an impulse, he turned to find out if the boys were following. To his deep regret, he noticed that many had stayed behind in the valley, while many others had turned back. Heartbroken, he wanted to retrace his steps to persuade those boys to follow him and to help them along, but he was absolutely forbidden to do so. "Those poor boys will be lost!" he protested.

"So much the worse for them," he was told. "They too received the call, but refused to follow you. They saw the road they had to travel. They had their chance."

Don Bosco insisted, pleaded and begged, but in vain.

"You too must obey," he was told. He had to walk on.

Innocence Lost

He was still smarting with this pain when he became aware of another sad fact: a large number of those riding in the wagon had gradually fallen off, so that a mere 150 still stood under the banner of innocence. His heart was aching with unbearable grief. He hoped that it was only a dream and made every effort to awaken himself, but unfortunately it was all too real. He clapped his hands and heard their sound; he groaned and heard his sighs resound through the room; he wanted to banish this horrible vision but could not.

"My dear boys," he exclaimed at this point of his narration, "I recognized those of you who stayed behind in the valley and those who turned back or fell from the wagon. I saw you all. You can be sure that I will do my utmost to save you. Many of you whom I urged to go to Confession did not accept my invitation. For heaven's sake, save your souls."

The Eighth Hill

Many of those who had fallen off the wagon joined those who were walking. Meanwhile, the singing in the wagon continued, and it was so sweet that it gradually abated Don Bosco's sorrow. Seven hills had already been climbed. As the boys reached the eighth, they found themselves in a wonderful village, where they stopped for a brief rest. The houses were indescribably beautiful and luxurious.

In telling the boys of this village, Don Bosco remarked: "I could repeat what St. Teresa said about heavenly things—*to speak of them is to belittle them.* They are just too beautiful for words. I shall only say that the doorposts of these houses seemed to be made of gold, crystal and diamond all at once. They were a most wonderful, satisfying, pleasing sight. The fields were dotted with trees laden simultaneously with blossoms, buds and fruit. It was out of this world!"

The boys scattered all over, eager to see everything and to taste the fruit. Here another surprise awaited Don Bosco. His boys suddenly looked like old men: toothless, wrinkled, white-haired, bent over, lame, leaning on canes. He was stunned, but the voice said: "Don't be surprised. It's been years and years since you left that valley. The music made your trip seem so short. If you want proof, look at yourself in the mirror and you will see that I am telling the truth." Don Bosco was handed a mirror. He himself had grown old, with his face deeply lined and his few remaining teeth decayed.

The march resumed. Now and then the boys asked to be allowed to stop and look at the novelties around them, but he kept urging them on. "We are neither hungry nor thirsty," he said. "We have no need to stop. Let us keep going!"

Far away, on the tenth hill, arose a light which grew increasingly larger and brighter, as though pouring from a gigantic doorway. Singing resumed, so enchanting that its like may possibly be enjoyed only in Paradise. It was simply indescribable, because it did not come from instruments or human throats. Don Bosco was so overjoyed that he awoke, only to find himself in bed.

He then explained his dream thus: *"The valley is this world; the bank symbolizes the obstacles we have to surmount in detaching ourselves from it*; the wagon is self-evident. The

---

P.S. For interpretations of this dream, read also Vol. VII, pages 470ff.

youngsters on foot were those who lost their innocence but repented of their sins." He also added that the ten hills symbolized the Ten Commandments, whose observance leads to eternal life. He concluded by saying that he was ready to tell some boys confidentially what they had been doing in the dream: whether they had remained in the valley or fallen off the wagon.

DEVILS
IN THE
CHURCH

22

(*Biographical Memoirs*, Vol. VI, page 627)

Don Bosco's persuasive words efficaciously helped new pupils to lay foundations for a fruitful school year (1861-1862). On November 28, as Fr. Ruffino relates, Don Bosco spoke to the boys as follows:

We dream when we sleep. Therefore, while I was sleeping, I found myself in church with all the boys. As Mass began, many red-robed, horned devils began circulating among the boys, trying to catch their attention with toys, books, delicacies, scenes of home and whatever each boy had a particular liking for. Every lad had a little devil at his side trying to distract him from the Mass. Little devils were perched on some boys' shoulders, petting and stroking them. As the bell signaled the Elevation, the boys bowed their heads and the devils disappeared. However, those lads who had devils on their shoulders turned their backs to the altar instead of adoring. After the Elevation, every devil was back to his job.

I believe, my dear boys, that this dream showed me all the distractions you are subjected to by the devil at Mass. The fact that some demons did not vanish at the Elevation means that those boys were in mortal sin. The devil no longer had to distract them; they are his already. He just keeps caressing them. Those boys can no longer even pray.

About a month later—on the last day of the year—Don

Bosco gave the boys the annual strenna for the new year, 1862. Fr. Bonetti's chronicle records the "Good Night" address as follows:

I decided to come down to see you and speak to you tonight because I knew that I would otherwise have to wait until next year. (Laughter). The year 1861 is passed. Those who spent it well will rejoice; others may feel sorrow and repent, but they will never get this year back again. *Fugit irreparabile tempus*—"Time flies irreparably." On the last night of each year, I usually give my sons a few suggestions for the new year. Here is what I recommend for the year 1862.

Do your utmost to hear the Mass devoutly; urge others to do the same. This year I very seriously want you to take this suggestion of mine to heart, because I really mean it. Great disasters loom over us. Holy Mass is *the* great means to appease God and avert His chastisement. Let us therefore carry out the wholesome advice of the Sacred Council of Trent: "*Let us always keep ourselves in the state of grace so as to be ready to receive Holy Communion when assisting at Mass, and thus more fully share in this august Sacrifice.*" (Vol. VI, page 631).

THE SNAKE AND THE ROSARY

23

(*Biographical Memoirs*, Vol. VII, pages 143-145)

We shall now draw from Francis Provera's notes:
"The life of a man upon earth is a warfare." (*Job* 7:1).
During these days Don Bosco received yet another proof of the devil's unceasing, devasting attacks against souls and of the need to repel him constantly and free his victims. By mid-August about 100 pupils had returned to the Oratory for summer school. At the "Good Night" address on August 20, 1862, Don Bosco, after giving some disciplinary reminders, addressed them as follows:

I want to tell you a dream I had some nights ago, most probably on the eve of the Assumption. I dreamed that I was at my brother's home at Castelnuovo d'Asti with all my boys. While they were at play, a total stranger came up to me and asked me to go with him. He took me to a meadow alongside the playground and pointed to a huge, ugly snake, over twenty feet long, coiled in the grass. Frightened, I wanted to run off, but the stranger held me back. "Get closer and take a good look," he said.

"What?" I gasped. "Don't you realize that the monster could spring on me and gobble me up in no time?" "Don't be afraid! Nothing of the sort will happen; just come with me."

"Nothing doing! I'm not crazy!"

"Then stay where you are," the stranger replied. And he

went to fetch a rope.

"Take this end," he said on his return, "and grip it tightly with both hands. I'll hold the other end, and we'll let it dangle over the snake."

"And then?"

"Then we'll snap it across its back."

"You must be crazy; the snake will leap up and tear us to pieces."

"No, it won't. Leave that to me."

"Count me out! I have no intention to risk my life for a thrill of this kind!"

Again I tried to run away, but the stranger once more assured me that I had nothing to fear, because the snake would do me no harm. He talked so persuasively that I stayed on and agreed to his plan. He went around to the other side of the monster. We stretched the rope and then snapped it across the snake's back. The monster immediately sprang up and struck at the rope, but as it did so, it ensnared itself as in a noose.

"Hold on!" the stranger shouted. "Don't let go!" He ran to a nearby pear tree and tied his end of the rope to it. Then he came to me and tied my end to the iron grating of a window in the house. The snake kept furiously struggling to free itself, writhing, thrashing and flailing about. In its fury, it tore itself to pieces, scattering its flesh over the area, till it was slashed to a mere skeleton.

The stranger then untied the rope and coiled it up. "Now watch very carefully!" he said as he put it into a box and closed it. By this time the boys had swarmed about me. Within a few moments he opened the box. We looked in and were astounded to see the rope shaped into the words *Ave Maria*— "Hail Mary."

"How did that happen?" I asked.

"The snake," the man replied, "is a symbol of the devil, whereas the rope stands for *Ave Maria*, or rather, the Rosary, a succession of Hail Marys with which we can strike, conquer and destroy all of Hell's demons."

What followed is even stranger and more amazing, but it's too late to tell you now. I'll leave it for tomorrow. In the meantime, let us give thought to what the stranger said about the Hail Mary and the Rosary. Let us devoutly say a Hail Mary whenever we are tempted, and we'll be sure to win. Good Night.

Part II
(page 416)

We read in the chronicle of Bro. Francis Provera:

On August 21, 1862, after night prayers, we were all anxious to hear the second part of the dream which Don Bosco had described as strange and interesting, but we were disappointed. "Last night," Don Bosco said, "I stated that I would tell you the second part of the dream, but regretfully I do not think it opportune to keep my promise . . ."

The following day, August 22, we again pestered him to tell us, at least privately, the part of the dream he had not revealed. He did not want to change his mind, but after much insistance on our part, he finally relented and promised that he would tell us more that evening. At the "Good Night" address, he spoke as follows:

Yielding to your repeated entreaties, I shall tell you the second part of the dream, or at least what little I can. First, I must make it clear that no one is to write or talk about it outside this house. Discuss it among yourselves, laugh at it, do as you wish, but only among yourselves.

Now, while talking with that stranger about the rope, the snake and what they symbolized, I turned around and saw boys picking up scraps of snake meat and eating them. "What are you doing?" I shouted. "Are you mad? That meat is poisonous."

"It's delicious!" They replied.

And yet no sooner had they swallowed it than they would

crumple to the ground, and their bodies would swell and harden like stone. I was helpless, because, despite this, more and more boys kept eating that meat. I shouted and yelled at them, and even slapped and punched them, to keep them from eating, but in vain. For every one who crumpled to the ground, another took his place. Then I called the clerics and told them to go among the boys and do all they could to make them stop eating that meat. My order was ineffective; worse yet, some clerics themselves began to eat it and they too fell to the ground.

Nearly out of my mind at seeing so many boys lying about me in such a pitiful state, I turned to the stranger. "What does this mean?" I asked. "These boys know that this meat will kill them, yet they eat it. Why?"

"Because 'the sensual man does not perceive the things that are of God!' That's why!" He answered.

"But isn't there some way of saving these boys?"

"Yes, there is."

"What?"

"Anvil and hammer."

"Anvil and hammer? What for?"

"To put the boys back in shape."

"You mean I am to put them on an anvil and strike them with the hammer?"

"Look," the stranger said, "this whole thing is a symbol. The hammer symbolizes Confession, and the anvil symbolizes Holy Communion. These are the remedies you must use."

I went to work and found the treatment very effective, but not for all. While most boys were restored to life and recovered, a few did not, because their Confessions were bad.

Among the remarks of the historian (pages 147-148) we read: "The poisonous meat of that monstrous snake might well symbolize scandal which destroys one's faith, or immoral, irreligious readings. Likewise, *what else might disobedience, collapsing, swelling up and hardening signify but pride, obstinacy and love of sin?*" The prayers and sacrifices of the just must first ask that God's grace warm hardened hearts and soften them, so that the Sacraments of Penance and Holy Eucharist may exercise their divine efficacy . . . Thus the hammer's blows and the anvil's support will both bring about the cure of an ulcer-ridden but now docile heart. As the sparks fly, the heart is reconditioned.

THE FOURTEEN TABLES

24

(*Biographical Memoirs*, Vol. VII, page 410f)

On August 5, 1860, Don Rua sang his first Solemn High Mass, assisted by Don Bosco. All day long, as "Vivas" were shouted to him, he kept trying to divert the cheers to Don Bosco. The day's celebration was a wonderful display of real brotherly love. No one who was not present can imagine the intense joy of all.

Don Bosco closed the celebration by telling the following dream at the "Good Night" address:

I saw my boys in a most gorgeous garden, seated at fourteen long tables arranged amphitheater-wise at three different terrace-like levels. The top-most tables were so lofty that they could hardly be seen.

At the very bottom, a certain number of boys were seated at a table which was bare except for bits of rancid, moldy bread mixed with garbage and husks. These poor boys looked like swine at their trough. I meant to tell them to throw that rubbish away, but instead I just asked them why they were served such loathsome refuse. They replied: "We have to eat the bread we have provided for ourselves. It's all we have."

This table symbolized the state of mortal sin. As Holy Scripture states: "They hated knowledge and chose not the fear of the Lord; they ignored My counsel, they spurned all My reproof . . . Now they eat the fruit of their own way, and with their own device be glutted." (*Prov.* 1:29-31).

As for the tables set on higher levels, the boys seated at them looked happier and ate better bread. They were very handsome, with a comliness and radiance constantly increasing. Their tables too were richly set with special linen, glittering candelabra, sparkling chinaware and indescribably gorgeous flowers. The platters held delicious foods and rare delicacies. The number of these boys was very great. These tables symbolized the state of repentant sinners.

Lastly, the table at the top had a sort of bread I cannot describe. It looked gold and red, as did the boys' garments and faces, which shone with brilliant light. All these boys looked radiantly happy; each one tried to share his joy with the others. Their comeliness and the glitter and splendor of their tables far surpassed all the others. These tables symbolized the state of those who had retained their baptismal innocence. As Holy Scripture says of the innocent and of the repentant sinner: "He who obeys me dwells in security, in peace, without fear of harm." (*Prov.* 1:33).

The most surprising aspect of this dream is that I knew each of the boys, so that as I see one of them now, I immediately seem to see him seated at one of those tables.

As I was entranced by that exceptional sight, I noticed a man some distance away. I ran to him to ask him questions, but I tripped on the way and awoke in my bed. You asked me to tell you a dream and I obliged. Give it no more importance than dreams deserve.

The following day Don Bosco told each boy privately at which table he was seated in the dream. To show them how high or low they stood, he graded them from the topmost table to the lowest. Asked if one could move from a lower to a higher table, he replied in the affirmative, except for the top-most table. Those who fell from that could not return, because that table was exclusively for those who had kept their baptismal innocence. Their number was small, whereas very many boys sat at the other tables. (Cf. page 411.)

A
LITTLE
MARMOT

25

(*Biographical Memoirs*, Vol. VI, page 160)

Don Bosco used to give a "short talk to the community" after night prayers, concluding always with the greeting of "Good Night." This tradition continues in Salesian schools, and the talk is called the "Good Night."

Here is the summary of one of the many "Good Nights" recorded in the volumes of the *Biographical Memoirs*:

One of the first "Good Nights" I heard from Don Bosco in 1859 was on the frequent reception of the Sacraments—a practice not yet generally taken up by the boys after their recent summer vacations. He narrated a dream in which he seemed to be standing near the Oratory main entrance while the boys returned from home. As they walked past him, he could see the state of their souls before God. A stranger also walked in with them, holding a small box. This stranger mingled with the boys, and when the time came for Confessions, he opened the box and, taking out a little marmot, started to give a puppet show of sorts. Rather than go to the church, the boys crowded around him to enjoy the fun, while he slowly withdrew into a corner of the playground farthest from the church.

Then, without naming anyone, Don Bosco proceeded to describe the spiritual condition of many boys. He also spoke of the devil's efforts and snares to distract and discourage them from Confession. His portrayal of the little marmot's tricks provoked many laughs, but it also made the boys reflect seriously on their spiritual condition—all the more so when later he told private inquirers things they thought nobody could ever know.

This dream was instrumental in inducing most of the boys to go to Confession much more frequently—generally, once a week; naturally, reception of Holy Communion became very frequent as well.

I also remember that once, as Don Bosco was talking of bodily health and of the important need of caring for it, the cleric Joseph Bongiovanni asked permission to speak. On being given leave, he said: "What are we to do, then, to enjoy good health and live a long life?"

Don Bosco replied: "I will give you a secret, or rather a prescription. While serving as a reply to the cleric Bongiovanni, it will also greatly benefit you all. *To enjoy good health and live a long life you need four things: 1. A clear conscience when you go to bed at night; that is, no fear of eternity. 2. Moderation in eating. 3. An active life. 4. Good companions, that is, fleeing from those who are corrupt."* He then briefly explained these four points.

As we can see, Don Bosco's "Good Nights" wisely governed the Oratory. One may read in that same chapter (22) some examples of Don Bosco's *kind firmness.*

A FIERCE DOG

26

(*Biographical Memoirs*, Vol. VII, page 391)

Fr. Ruffino narrates in the chronicle of April 1864:

At this time there was a boy at the Oratory named P _____ who would have nothing to do with Sacraments or prayers. He was there by force. One day Don Bosco took him aside.

"Why is it there is always a fierce dog snarling and snapping at you? he asked him.

"I don't see any dog."

"I do! Tell me, how does your conscience feel?" The boy hung his head.

"Take heart," Don Bosco went on. "Come with me and everything will be all right."

The youngster became Don Bosco's friend and is now determined to do good.

At the spiritual retreat's close on the evening of April 13, Don Bosco expressed his regret that some boys had not used it for the good of their souls. "During these few days," he said, "I saw all the sins of each of you clearly as if they were written in front of me. There was some confusion only when a few, in making their General Confession, tried to tell me their sins instead of answering my questions. This was a singular grace the Lord gave me during these few days for your own good. Now most probably, the few who did not follow my advice will ask me whether I can still read their conscience, and the answer, unfortunately, is no. They have lost their chance!"

A GIANT MASTIFF

27

(*Biographical Memoirs*, Vol. VII, page 125)

In July 1862, Don Bosco spoke about sacrilegious Confessions of boys deliberately concealing mortal sins. He clarified his point with the following personal incident:

One night, I dreamed of a boy. His heart was being eaten up by worms as he tried to pluck them out. I paid no attention to the dream; but the following night I again saw this boy. Now a giant mastiff straddled him, gnawing away his heart. I was sure that the Lord had some special grace in store for this boy, whose conscience must have been badly muddled. I kept an eye on him. One day I cornered him.

"Would you do me a favor?" I asked.

"Sure, if I can."

"You can, if you want to."

"What is it?"

"Will you really do it?"

"Yes, I will."

"Tell me, have you ever kept anything back in Confession?"

He was about to deny it, but I immediately added: "Why don't you confess this and that?" He glanced at me and burst into tears. "It's true," he said, "it's years since I wanted to confess that, but I'm too scared." I comforted him and told him how he could make peace with God.

CONSCIENCES REVEALED 28

(*Biographical Memoirs*, Vol. VI, page 478)

For three consecutive nights, I found myself in the countryside of Rivalta with Fr. Joseph Cafasso, Silvio Pellico[1] and Count Charles Cays.[2] The first night we discussed current religious topics; the second night we debated and solved moral cases relevant to the spiritual direction of young people. After having the same dream twice, I decided I would tell you about it, if it came to me again. Sure enough, on the night of December 30, I found myself once more with the same people in the same place. Putting other matters aside, I recalled that the following night, the last of the year, I would have to give

---

1. Silvio Pellico (1789-1854), a Piedmontese patriot, spent most of his early adult life in Milan, where he joined the "Carbonari," a secret society working for Italy's independence. Arrested by the Austrians, who then ruled Lombardy, he was sentenced to twenty years of hard labor. Pardoned in 1830, he returned to Turin. Up to his imprisonment, Pellico had been a lukewarm Catholic, but in the distress of prison life, he resolved to love God and his fellow men. In 1832 he wrote the story of his prison life, *Le Mie Prigioni*, which became the most famous book in the literature of the "Risorgimento." At this time he was employed as secretary to Marchioness Barolo in Turin.

2. Born in Turin on November 24, 1813, Count Cays attended the local Jesuit secondary school and later obtained his doctorate in law at the University of Turin. He married and had two children, but became a widower at the age of 32. From 1857 to 1860 he was a deputy in the Piedmontese Parliament and courageously defended the Church's rights against the anticlericals. In 1877 he became a Salesian; ordained a priest a year later, he continued to render invaluable assistance to Don Bosco. He died at the Oratory on October 4, 1882, at the age of 69, as he himself had predicted.

you the customary strenna for the New Year. Therefore, I turned to Fr. Cafasso and said: "Father, since you are such a dear friend of mine, please give me the strenna for my boys."

"On one condition," he replied: "First you must tell them to put their accounts in order."

We were standing in a large room with a table in the center. Fr. Cafasso, Silvio Pellico and Count Cays sat themselves at the table. As I had been requested by Fr. Cafasso, I went out to get my boys. They were all busy adding up figures on a tablet. As I called them one by one, they presented their papers to the above-named gentlemen, who checked the sums and either approved or rejected them. Quite a few boys were turned back, sad and worried. Those whose totals had been found correct were quite happy and ran out to play. Since the line of boys was long, the examination took some time, but eventually it came to an end, or so it seemed to me, until I noticed that some boys were still standing outside and were not coming in.

"Why don't they come in?" I asked Fr. Cafasso.

"Their tablets are perfect blanks," he replied. "They have no totals to show us. This is a question of summing up all that one has done. Let them add up whatever they have done and we'll verify the totals."

After all the accounts had been checked, I went outside with the three gentlemen. All the boys whose totals had been found correct were running about having a joyful time, as happy as could be. You cannot imagine how that sight cheered me. Some boys, though, just stood apart, wistfully watching the games. Some were blindfolded; others had a mist about their eyes or a dark cloud around their heads. Smoke came from the heads of some, others had a head full of clay, or empty of the things of God. I recognized each boy. So clear is the picture in my mind now that I can name each one. I soon realized too that many boys were missing. "Where are those boys who had blank tables?" I wondered. I looked for them, but in vain. Finally, I spotted some boys in a distant corner of the playground. What a wretched sight they were!

One lad was stretched out on the ground with the pallor of death; others were seated on a low, filthy bench; still others were resting on dirty straw mattresses or on the hard, bare ground. These were the boys whose totals had not been approved. They had various diseases: their tongues, ears and eyes were swarming with worms that ate into them. One boy had a rotting tongue; another's mouth was crammed with mud; a third's breath was foul with pestilence. Other diseases afflicted the rest. One boy's heart was moth-eaten; another's was rotted away; others had all kinds of sores. One lad's heart seemed to be all chewed up. The whole scene was a veritable hospital.

The sight shocked me, and I could not believe my eyes. "How can this be?" I kept asking myself. I went up to one boy and asked.

"Are you really so and so?"

"Yes," he replied, "that's me."

"What happened to you?"

"It's my own doing, flour from my own grist. I reaped what I planted!"

I questioned another boy and got the same reply. I felt terribly hurt, but was soon to be comforted by what I am about to tell you.

Meanwhile, pitying these boys, I turned to Fr. Cafasso and begged for a remedy. "You know what must be done just as well as I," he replied. "Figure it out for yourself."

"At least give me a strenna for the healthy ones," I insisted humbly but trustfully.

Beckoning me to follow, he went back to the mansion and opened a door leading into a spectacular hall which was richly draped, glittering with gold and silver. Dazzling chandeliers of a thousand lights flooded it with blinding radiance. As far as the eye could see, it stretched endlessly in length and breadth. In its center stood a giant table laden with all kinds of sweets, oversized bittersweet cookies and biscuits. Any one delicacy alone would have satisfied a person. At the sight, I impulsively made as if to run and call my boys to enjoy this bonanza, but Fr. Cafasso stopped me. "Wait!" he said. "Not everyone may enjoy these sweets, but only those whose totals were approved."

Even so, the hall was quickly filled with boys. I started breaking up and handing out the cookies and biscuits, but again Fr. Cafasso objected. "Not everyone here may have those," he said. "Not all deserve them." And he pointed some boys out to me: those whose totals had been approved, but who had a mist over their eyes or clay in their hearts, or whose hearts were empty of the things of God. These too were excluded, just as those with sores who had not been allowed into the hall.

I immediately begged Fr. Cafasso to let me give them some of the sweets, too. "They are also my dear children," I said. "And besides, there is plenty."

"No," he repeated firmly. "Only the healthy ones can savor these sweets. The others have no taste for these delicacies. They would only get sick."

I said no more and began serving those who had been pointed out to me. When I was through, I gave out another generous helping to all of them. I must say that I really enjoyed seeing the boys eat with such relish. Joy shone on their faces and so transfigured them that they did not look like the same boys any more.

The lads in the hall who had not been allowed to have any sweets stood in a corner. I felt so sorry for them that again I begged Fr. Cafasso to let me give them some also.

"No," he replied. "Not yet. Make them get well first." I kept looking at them, as well as at the many others outside. I knew them all. I also noticed that, to make matters worse, some had moth-eaten hearts. Turning to Fr. Cafasso, I said: "Won't you please tell me what medicine to give them?" Again he replied: "Figure it out for yourself. You know what to do!"

Again I asked him for a strenna to give all the boys.

"Very well," he answered. "I'll give you one." Turning about as if to leave, he exclaimed three times, each time in a louder voice: "Watch out! Watch out! Watch out!" With these words he and his companions vanished. I woke up and found myself sitting in bed. My shoulders were as cold as ice.

That's my dream. Make of it what you like. It's just a dream, but if anything in it is good for our souls, let's take it. However, I would not want you to talk about it with outsiders. I told it to you because you are my children. I positively do not want you to tell it to others.

Meanwhile, I assure you, I have you all present in my mind as I saw you in the dream, and I can tell who was diseased and who was not, who was eating those sweets and who was not. I am not going to disclose each boy's condition here, but I will do so privately.

Now here is the strenna for the New Year: *"Frequent and sincere Confession, frequent and devout Communion."*

P.S. A note by the historian:

In this dream Fr. Cafasso seems to judge on matters concerning religion and morality; Silvio Pellico (a scholar, writer and politician) on matters concerning scholastic and professional duties; Count Cays (a learned, holy nobleman who became a Salesian at age 60) on matters concerning discipline.

Sweet biscuits seem to signify the food of those who have just begun to serve the Lord; amaretti (bitterish cookies) are for those who have advanced on the way of perfection.

A PACK OF MONSTERS **29**

(*Biographical Memoirs*, Vol. VIII, page 32)

On February 24, 1865, after having told the community why he had been away for a few days at Cuneo, where he had stayed with the bishop, he went on to narrate the following dream:

The first night I went to bed towards eleven and fell asleep immediately. As usual, I began to dream, and since the tongue always turns to the aching tooth, as the saying goes, I dreamed that I was at the Oratory with my beloved boys. I seemed to be seated at my desk while you were having a world of fun playing, shouting and running about. I was very pleased with all the noise, because I know that when you are playing, the devil has no chance to harm you, no matter how hard he tries. I was rejoicing at this hubbub, when suddenly all noise ceased and a deadly silence fell upon the playground. In alarm I stood up to find out what had happened.

As I crossed into the waiting room, a horrid monster burst in from the outer door. Seemingly unaware of my presence, head and eyes lowered to the ground, the monster advanced straight forward like a beast about to spring on its victim. Trembling for your safety, I looked down from the window to see if anything had happened to you. The whole playground was full of monsters like the one in my waiting room, though smaller. You, my boys, had been forced back against the walls and porticos, but many of you were lying on the ground, seemingly dead. This piteous sight so frightened me that I awoke screaming. I woke everybody else up too, from the bishop to the last servant.

My dear boys, generally speaking we must pay no attention to dreams, but when they teach us a moral lesson, we may give them a thought. I have always tried to learn why certain things happen, and I'll do so also as regards this dream. That monster may well be the devil, who is ever trying to ruin us. Some boys fell victims to him, while others went unscathed. Shall I show you how not to fear him and successfully withstand him?

Listen: *there are two things the devil is deadly afraid of: fervent Communions and frequent visits to the Blessed Sacrament.*

Do you want Our Lord to grant you *many* graces?

Visit Him *often.*

Do you want Him to grant you *only a few?*

Visit Him but *seldom.*

Do you want the devil to *attack you?*

Rarely visit the Blessed Sacrament.

Do you want the devil to *flee from you?*

Visit Jesus *often.*

Do you want to *overcome* the devil?

Take refuge *at Jesus' feet.*

Do you want *to be overcome* by the devil?

Give up visiting Jesus.

Visiting the Blessed Sacrament is essential, my dear boys, if you want to overcome the devil. Therefore, make frequent visits to Jesus. If you do that, the devil will never prevail against you.

(*Biographical Memoirs*, Vol. VII, pp. 128-131)

July 1862 was marked by further amazing events center-
ing on Don Bosco. The Ruffino chronicle has this entry: "July
1, 1862. After dinner today, Don Bosco remarked to a few
around him: 'We shall have a funeral this month.' He repeated
this later on, but always to only a few."

These confidential disclosures keenly excited the clerics'
curiosity, and so, during recreation, unless assigned elsewhere,
they would cluster around Don Bosco, hoping to pick up other
startling bits of information. One such fact they learned in
this way was a plan to open girls' schools also. Both John
Bonetti and Caesar Chiala recorded this in writing.

On July 6, Don Bosco narrated a dream he had had the
night before. His audience consisted of Fr. John Baptist
Francesia, Fr. Angelo Savio, Fr. Michael Rua, Francis Cer-
ruti, Bartholomew Fusero, John Bonetti, Chevalier Frederick
Oreglia, John Baptist Anfossi, Celestine Durando, Francis
Provera and a few others. He spoke as follows:

Last night I had a strange dream. With Marchioness Barolo,[1]
I seemed to be strolling about a small plaza, which opened
into a vast plain where the Oratory boys were happily playing. As I respectfully attempted to move to her left, she
stopped me, saying: "No, stay where you are." She then began

---

1. Marchioness Juliette Colbert Barolo (1785-1864).

talking about my boys. "It's wonderful that you look after boys," she said. "Let me care for the girls. Leave that to me, so that there'll be no disagreements."

"Well," I replied, "didn't Our Lord come into this world to redeem both boys and girls?"

"Of course," she replied.

"Then I must see to it that His Blood be not uselessly shed for either group."

As we were thus talking, an eerie silence suddenly fell over the boys. They stopped playing and, looking very frightened, fled helter-skelter. The Marchioness and I stood still for a moment and then rushed to learn what had caused the scare. Suddenly, at the far end of the plain, I saw an enormous horse alight upon the ground. So huge was the animal that my blood ran cold.

"Was the horse as big as this room?" Fr. Francesia asked.

"Oh, much bigger! It was truly a monstrous thing—three or four times the size of Palazzo Madama.[2] Marchioness Barolo fainted at the sight. I myself was so shaken up that I could barely stand. In my fright I took shelter behind a nearby house, but the owners drove me off. "Go away!" they screamed. "Go away!" Meanwhile, I kept thinking: "What can this horse be? I must stop running and try to get a close look at it." Still quaking with fear, I pulled myself together and, retracing my steps, walked toward the beast. What a horror to see those ears and that frightful snout! At times it seemed to be carrying a load of riders; at other times it seemed to have wings. "It must be a demon!" I exclaimed.

Others were with me. "What kind of monster is this?" I

---

2. Palazzo Madama, located in the center of Piazza Castello in the heart of Turin, is a massive building consisting of three structures of different origin—Roman, medieval, and modern—summing up the city's two thousand years of history. Its magnificent internal staircase and eighteenth-century façade by Filippo Juvarra represent one of the finest creations of European baroque. Palazzo Madama was the seat of the Subalpine Senate from 1840 to 1860 and of the Italian Senate until 1864. At present it houses the City Museum of Ancient Art.

asked one of them.

"The red horse of the Apocalypse," he replied.

At this point I awoke in a cold sweat and found myself in bed. Throughout the morning, as I said Mass or heard Confessions, that beast kept haunting me. Now I would like someone to check if a red horse is really mentioned in the Scriptures and find out what it stands for.

Celestine Durando was chosen to do the research. Fr. M. Rua, though, remarked that a red horse—symbol of bloody persecution against the Church, according to Martini,[3] is indeed mentioned in the Apocalypse, Chapter 6, verse 3-4: "And when he opened the sacred seal, I heard the second living creature saying, 'Come.' *And there went forth another horse, a red one; and to him who was sitting on it, was given to take peace from the earth, and that men should slay one another, and there was given to him a great sword."*

Perhaps in Don Bosco's dream the red horse symbolized contemporary (European) godless democracy which, fuming against the Church, was steadily making headway to the detriment of the social order and gaining control over national and local governments, education and the courts.

Its goal was to complete the destruction of the right of ownership of every religious society and charitable institution, which had been started by conniving national governments. Don Bosco used to remark: "To prevent this calamity, all the faithful, and we too in our small way, must zealously and courageously strive to halt this unbridled monster."

How? By alerting the masses to its false teachings through the practice of charity and wholesome publications and by turning their minds and hearts to St. Peter's Chair—the unshakable foundation of all God-given authority, the master key of all social order, the immutable charter of man's duties

---

3. Antonio Martini (1720-1809), Archbishop of Florence, translated the New Testament from Greek and the Old Testament from the Vulgate into Italian. His version became most popular in Italy.

and rights, the divine light which unmasks the deception of evil passions, the faithful and powerful guardian of natural and Christian morality, the irrevocable guarantor of eternal reward and punishment. The Church, St. Peter's Chair and the Pope are one and the same thing. That is why Don Bosco wanted an all-out effort to make these truths accepted. His goals were to fully document the incalculable benefits brought by popes to civil society, to rebut all slanders hurled against them and to foster gratitude, loyalty and love for them.

This was Don Bosco's attitude. In his love of the Sovereign Pontiff, he was truly great, both in word and in deed. He used to say that he could kiss each page of Salzano's Church History, because this Italian historian had clearly shown therein his love for the popes. To his clerics he gave a practical rule of thumb in appraising a book: "If its author is somewhat unfavorable to the Pope, don't read the book."

The Bonetti chronicle had this entry for this same year, 1862:

"When Don Bosco talks about the popes, he can go on forever. He always has new praises for them and speaks so charmingly as to inflame his listeners. He is at his best in two subjects: the virtue of purity and the papacy. He entrances and amazes everyone. To believe this, one must only read his works, especially his *Lives of the Popes,* which we consider required reading for anyone chosen by Providence to write the biography of this faithful servant of God."

The Mystery of Iniquity

In the following pages (dreams of the toad, the vine and Hell), you will find Don Bosco engaged in the fight against a mysterious power that plays havoc among the children of men. You will find a horrible monster, a most disgusting toad as large as a bull, that wants to devour Don Bosco himself. But in the name of God, by repeated Signs of the Cross and through holy water and loud cries, Don Bosco puts it to flight.

It is not easy to overcome Satan. One must have courage and strength. Faith gives us strength. But remember well that Satan cannot do anything against us, unless we accept him. However, human weakness is great. Let us never trust ourselves, because the wicked one can well choose every weakness on our part.

Satan exists, Hell exists. The mission of Jesus Christ is an all-out war against the Power of Darkness.

Don Bosco was reluctant to narrate those dreadful dreams. But a voice from on high tells him distinctly: "Why don't you speak? Tell them. . ."

"Therefore it is the will of God that I tell you what I have seen," said Don Bosco.

This is a clear warning for educators. One must speak: Hell exists and many fall into it. Truth will put Satan to flight.

A MYSTERIOUS VINE

31

(*Biographical Memoirs*, Vol. IX, Ch. 75)

A Horrible Monster

My dear boys, last night I said that I had something unpleasant to tell you. It's a dream I had. I was not going to talk about it, because I thought it was nothing but a dream and because, whenever I have narrated my dreams, remarks and objections have been made. Now, however, a second dream forces me to reveal the first, and all the more so considering that for the past few nights—particularly the last three nights—I have been repeatedly troubled by nightmares. You know that I went to Lanzo for a little rest. Well, on my last night there, no sooner had I fallen asleep than I dreamed that I saw a most loathsome toad, huge as an ox, enter my room and squat at the foot of my bed. I stared breathlessly as its legs, body and head swelled and grew more and more repugnant; its green body, fiery eyes, red-lined mouth and throat, and small bony ears presented a terrifying sight. Staring wildly, I kept muttering to myself: "But a toad has no ears." I also noticed two horns jutting from its snout and two greenish wings sprouting from its sides. Its legs looked like those of a lion, and its long tail ended in a forked tip.

At the moment, I seemed not a bit afraid; but when that monster began edging closer to me, opening its huge, tooth-studded jaws, I really became terribly frightened. I thought it was a demon from Hell, because it looked like one. I made the Sign of the Cross, but nothing happened. I rang the bell, but no one responded. I shouted, but in vain. The monster would not retreat. "What do you want of me, you ugly devil?" I asked. As if in answer, it just crept forward, ears fully stretched out and pointing upward. Then, resting its front paws on the top of the bedstead and raising itself on its hind legs, it paused momentarily, looked at me and crawled forward on my bed until its snout was close to my face. I felt such revulsion that I tried to jump out of bed, but just then the monster opened its jaws wide. I wanted to defend myself and shove the monster back, but it was so hideous that, even in my predicament, I did not dare to touch it. I screamed and frenziedly reached behind me for the small holy water font, but I only hit the wall. Meanwhile, the monstrous toad had managed to mouth my head, so that half of my body was inside its foul jaws. "In the name of God," I shouted, "why are you doing this to me?" At these words, the toad drew back and let my head free. Again I made the Sign of the Cross, and since I had now dipped my hand in the holy water font, I flung a few drops of water at the monster. With a frightening shriek it fell backward and vanished, while a mysterious voice from on high clearly said: "Why don't you tell them?"

The director of Lanzo, Fr. Lemoyne, awakened by my prolonged shrieks, heard my pounding on the wall. "Don Bosco" he asked me in the morning, "were you having nightmares last night?"

"Why do you ask?"

"Because I heard your screams."

I realized that God willed I should reveal what I had seen. For this reason, and to rid myself of these nightmares, I have decided to tell you everything. Let us thank the Lord for His mercy. Meanwhile, let us strive to carry out His admonitions, no matter what way He may choose to make them known to us; and let us use the means He sends to enable us to save our souls. Through these dreams I have come to know the state of conscience of each of you.

I wish, though, that you keep within these walls what I am

going to disclose to you. I beg you not to write about it or talk about it outside the house, because such things are not to be ridiculed, as some people might do, and also because I want to avoid possible unpleasant complications. I tell you these things confidentially, as father to his beloved sons, and you should listen as though it were your own father telling them to you. Well then, here are the dreams which I would rather forget, but must reveal.

I began to have these dreams on Sunday, April 5, at the very beginning of Holy Week, and this went on for several miserable nights. These dreams so exhausted me that in the morning I felt more done in than if I had been working all night. They also alarmed and upset me very much. The first night I dreamed that I was dead; the second, that I was standing at God's judgment seat to settle my accounts. After each dream I awoke to realize that I was alive and had time to prepare better for a holy death. The third night I dreamed that I was in Heaven. I surely enjoyed that, but it all vanished when I woke up the next morning. I nevertheless felt determined, no matter what the cost, to gain the Eternal Kingdom which I had glimpsed. So far these dreams did not concern you in the least and would have meant nothing to you. When one falls asleep with something on his mind, his imagination goes to work and he dreams about it.

The Mysterious Vine

The dream of the mysterious vine is a parable.
Part I. *The States of Conscience.*

a) All leaves only. Semblance of good works. In reality, zero. It symbolizes the boys who do not aim at pleasing God.
b) Big bunches of ripe grapes, but of a rotten taste. Sin spoils the heart. Sadness comes after sin. The grace of God and conscience will cure them.
c) Handsome clusters of ruddy grapes. It symbolizes the boys

(too few, unfortunately) who correspond to the care bestowed on them. Boys radiant with joy.

Anyway, I had another dream, and this is the one I must tell you. The night of Holy Thursday (April 9) I had hardly dozed off, when I dreamed I was standing in these porticoes with our priests, clerics and boys around me. Then all of you vanished, and I seemed to step into the playground with only Fr. Rua, Fr. Cagliero, Fr. Francesia, Fr. Savio and young Preti. A little distance away stood Joseph Buzzetti and Fr. Stephen Rumi, a good friend of ours from the Genoa seminary.

Suddenly, the Oratory, as we now know it, changed its appearance and looked as it had been in its very beginning, when only those just mentioned were there. At that time our playground adjoined vast, untilled fields stretching up to the citadel meadows where our boys often strayed in their games.

We sat near the present cabinet shop under my bedroom window, where once we had a vegetable garden, and began talking about the house and the boys. Suddenly, a gorgeous vine—the very one that used to be there—sprouted out of the ground in front of this pillar supporting the water fountain near the entrance of the old Pinardi shed. (The platform on which Don Bosco was standing was backed against this pillar.) We were astonished at the appearance of the vine after so many years, and we wondered how it could have happened. Meanwhile, the vine kept growing to about a man's height, spreading countless shoots and tendrils into all directions, until it covered the entire playground and stretched beyond it. Oddly, its shoots did not grow upward, but spread out parallel to the ground like a very vast arbor with no visible support. Its budding leaves were a deep green, and its shoots were astonishingly healthy and strong. Soon handsome clusters of grapes broke out, grew in size and took on a purplish-red color.

"How can this vine have grown so quickly?" we asked each other in amazement. "What does it all mean?"

"Let's wait and see," I replied.

I kept watching the vine most carefully, when suddenly all the grapes fell to the ground and turned into a crowd of lively, cheerful boys. In no time the whole playground and the area covered by the vine were filled with boys who were jumping about, playing and having a grand time. It was a sight to behold. There, under that unusual arbor, I could see all the boys who have been, are, or will be at the Oratory and in other Salesian schools. Very many were unknown to me.

You know that a guide always shows up in my dreams. Well, at this point a stranger appeared at my side and stood watching the boys with me. Then a mysterious curtain abruptly appeared before us, blotting out this joyous scene.

No higher than the vine itself, this curtain in its entire width seemed to be hanging from the shoots of the vine like a stage curtain. All we could see now was the upper part of the vine stretched out like an enormous green carpet. In the meantime, the boys' cheerful hubbub had quickly turned into gloomy silence.

The Vine with Nothing but Leaves

"Look!" the guide told me, pointing to the vine.

I got closer. The lovely grape-laden vine had now nothing but leaves, bearing this inscription: *Nihil invent ea!*—"He found nothing on it!" *(Matt.* 21:19). Puzzled as to its significance, I asked my guide: "Who are you? What does this vine symbolize?"

In answer, he parted the curtain. Only a portion of the great many boys I had seen before were there now, most of them unknown to me.

"These boys," he explained, "have plenty of opportunities for doing good, but they do not aim at pleasing God. They make believe they are doing good to keep up appearances, they painstakingly obey house rules to avoid reprimands or loss of esteem and are respectful toward superiors, but they do not profit by their teachings, exhortations or efforts. All these boys strive for is some prominent, money-making position in the world. They have no concern to discover their vocation, they readily reject the Lord's call, while they keep disguising their intentions lest they lose any advantage. In short, they are those who do things out of necessity and derive no good for eternity."

How disappointed I was to see in that group several boys whom I believed to be very good, affectionate and sincere!

The Vine with Rotten Grapes

"Unfortunately, this is not all," my guide continued, letting go of the curtain. "Look up there now." And he pointed to the upper part of the arbor.

Among the leaves I could see clusters of grapes that looked very tasty. Happily, I got closer and noticed that the grapes were pockmarked, over-ripe, moldy, wormy, pecked, rotten or were shriveled—a total disaster. Their stench fouled the air.

Again the stranger lifted the curtain. "Look," he said. I saw another throng of boys, but not the countless number as at the beginning of the dream. Formerly very handsome, they now appeared ugly, sullen and covered with hideous sores, and they walked about with great melancholy as if stooped or wasted by age. No one spoke. All were past, present and future pupils of ours. The last mentioned were the most numerous. They all looked dejected and did not dare raise their eyes.

My companions and I were dismayed and speechless. "What happened?" I finally asked my guide. "These boys, once so handsome and joyful—why are they now so ugly and melancholy?"

"Because of their sins," was the answer. And as these boys were walking past me, he added, "Take a good look at them."

I noticed then that their foreheads and hands bore the name of each boy's sin. To my great surprise, I recognized several boys. I had always believed them to be very virtuous; now I was discovering that hideous sores were festering in their souls.

As they filed past, I could read on their foreheads: Immodesty, Scandal, Malevolence, Pride, Idleness, Gluttony, Envy, Anger, Vindictiveness, Blasphemy, Impiety, Disobedience, Sacrilege, Theft.

"Not all the boys are as you see them now," my guide remarked. "But they will be so one day if they do not change their ways. Many of these sins are not serious in themselves, but they will lead to serious falls and eternal perdition. *Qui spernit modica, paulatim decidet*—"He who despises trifles will sink down little by little." (*Ecclus.* 19:1). Gluttony breeds impurity; contempt for superiors leads to contempt for priests and the Church, and so on!

Downhearted at such a sight, I took my notebook and pencil to jot down the names of the boys I knew and their sins— or at least their predominant sin—so that I might warn and correct them. But the guide held my arm. "What are you trying to do?" he asked.

"I want to jot down what's written on their foreheads in order to warn them so that they may amend their lives."

"You may not do that."

"Why not?"

"They have all they need to go through life unscathed. They have house rules; let them observe them. They have superiors; let them obey them. They have the Sacraments; let them receive them. They have Penance; let them not profane it by concealing different sins. They have the Holy Eucharist; let them not partake of it in the state of mortal sin. Let them check their eyes, avoid bad companions, bad books, foul conversations, and so on. Keeping the house rules will save them. Let them promptly obey; let them stop trying to fool their teachers so as to idle away their time. Let them willingly obey their superiors instead of looking upon them as boresome watchdogs, self-interested counselors or even enemies. Let them not consider it a great victory when they succeed

in concealing their wrong-doings and escaping punishment.
Let them be reverent in church and pray willingly and
devoutly, without disturbing others or chattering. Let them
study when it's time to study, work when it's time to work
and behave at all times. Study, work and prayer are the things
that will keep them good."

Notwithstanding his prohibition, I kept pestering my guide
to let me write down the boys' names. At this, he snatched
my notebook and threw it on the ground, saying: "For the
last time, I say there is no need to write down their names.
God's grace and the voice of conscience will tell your boys
what not to do."

"Does this mean," I asked, "that I cannot tell my dear boys
anything of what I have seen? Have you any suggestion for
them?"

"You may tell them whatever you will remember," he
replied.

The Vine with Ripe, Ruddy Grapes

He again let the curtain drop and once more we saw the
vine. Its nearly leafless shoots held handsome clusters of
ruddy, full-grown grapes. I went closer and found them to be
as good as they looked. Their delightful sight and pleasant
smell made my mouth water.

Again, my guide lifted the curtain. Under that arbor I once
more saw many boys—our present, past and future pupils.
They were handsome beyond compare and radiant with joy.

"These," the stranger explained, "are the boys who, thanks
to your care, are yielding or will yield good fruit. They are
those who practice virtue and will greatly console you."

Delighted though I was, I somehow also felt grieved that
their number was not as great as I had hoped.

As I stood watching them, the bell rang and the boys left.
The clerics who were with me went to their tasks. I looked
about me and found myself alone. The vine was gone and

my guide had vanished. At this point I woke up and was able to get a little rest.

On Friday, May 1, Don Bosco continued his narrative:

As I told you last night, I awoke thinking I had heard the bell ring, but then I returned to sleep. Suddenly, somebody shook me. I found myself in my room, answering my mail. Afterward, I walked to the balcony, gazed for a moment at the majestic dome of our new church and then went downstairs and stepped into the porticoes. At short intervals, priests and clerics came from their various assignments and crowded around me, among them Fr. Rua, Fr. Cagliero, Fr. Francesia and Fr. Savio.

More Rotten Grapes

As I stood chatting with them, the Church of Mary, Help of Christians and all our present buildings abruptly disappeared, and we found ourselves in front of the old Pinardi shed. As in the previous dream, a vine sprouted up in exactly the same place, as if from the same roots, grew to the same height and then spread its shoots horizontally throughout a vast area. The shoots in turn sprouted leaves; then there came clusters of grapes that ripened under my very eyes. But no boys were to be seen. The bunches of grapes were truly enormous, like those of the Promised Land. One of them would have taxed the strength of a man. The perfectly ripe, golden grapes were oblong and extraordinarily large, so that a single one would have been quite a mouthful. Briefly, they looked so good as to make one's mouth water. "Eat me," they seemed to say.

Fr. Cagliero and the other priests marveled, while I kept exclaiming, "How gorgeous they are!"

Unceremoniously, Fr. Cagliero plucked a few grapes and put one in his mouth. No sooner did he sink his teeth into it than he spat it out so forcefully that we thought he was vomiting. The grape had the taste of a rotten egg. "Goodness gracious," he exclaimed after much spitting. "What stuff, it's enough to kill a man."

We all stood speechless. At this moment, a serious-looking man came out of the sacristy of the old chapel and determinedly strode up to me.

"How can such beautiful grapes taste so rotten?" I asked him. As if in answer, he gravely fetched a bundle of sticks, picked a well-knotted one and offered it to Fr. Savio, saying: "Take this and thrash these shoots." Fr. Savio refused and stepped back. The man then approached Fr. Francesia, but he too declined. The stranger then turned to Fr. Cagliero and, taking him by the arm, tried to press the stick in his hand. "Take it and strike," he said. "Thrash and knock down." So saying, he pointed to a certain spot. Startled, Fr. Cagliero stepped back. "Are you joking?" he exclaimed, striking his fist into his other hand. But the stranger insisted: "Take it and strike." "Not I," Fr. Cagliero shot back. Then he hid behind me in fright.

Foiled but unperturbed, the stranger turned to Fr. Rua who, like Fr. Cagliero, took refuge behind me. The man then came up to me. "Take this stick and strike those shoots," he commanded. I made a great effort to see whether I was dreaming or awake, but it all seemed very real to me.

"Who are you?" I asked. "Why must I knock these shoots to the ground? Am I dreaming? Am I imagining things? Are you speaking to me in God's name?"

"Draw closer to the vine," he answered, "and see what's written on those leaves." I complied and read: *Ut quid terram occupat?*—"Why does it still encumber the ground?" (*Luke* 13:7).

"That's from the Gospel," my guide exclaimed.

"Yes," I remarked, "but remember that in the Gospel we also read that Our Lord allowed the vine-dresser to dig around it and manure it, putting off its destruction until every attempt had been made to help it bear good fruit."

"All right. We will postpone the punishment. Meanwhile, take a look." So saying, he pointed to the vine. I looked, but I could not understand what he was driving at.

"Come here," he said, "and read what's written on the grapes."

I noticed then that they bore the name of each pupil and his predominant sin. I was aghast at what I saw. I was particularly frightened by such inscriptions: *"Proud, Unfaithful to his Promises, Unchaste, Two-Faced, Neglectful of His Duties, Calumniator, Vindictive, Heartless, Sacrilegious, Contemptuous of Authority, Stumbling Block, Follower of False Doctrines."* I saw the names of those *quorum deus venter est*—"whose god is their belly;" of those who *scientia inflat*—"are bloated by knowledge;" of those who *quaerunt quae sua sunt, non quae Jesus Christi*—"seek their own interests, not Our Lord's;" of those who scheme against their superiors and the house rules. Those names identified past, present and future pupils of ours. The last mentioned—quite a number of them—were unknown to me.

"This is the fruit we get from this vineyard," the man said gravely—"bitter, bad and harmful to eternal salvation."

I immediately tried to jot down some names in my notebook, but again my guide stopped me. "What are you up to do?" he asked.

"Please, let me take down the names of those I know, so that I may warn them privately and correct them," I pleaded.

It was no use. He would not consent.

"If I tell my boys the pitiful state they are in, they will amend their lives," I insisted.

"If they do not believe the Gospel," he replied, "they won't believe you either."

I kept insisting that I wanted to take some notes for the future, but ignoring me, he walked up to Fr. Rua with the bundle of sticks.

"Take one," he told him, "and strike the vine." Crossing his arms, Fr. Rua bowed his head and, murmuring "Patience," glanced at me. I nodded approval.

Fr. Rua then grabbed a stick, got close to the vine, and began to beat it at the spot indicated. He had hardly dealt a blow when the guide motioned him to stop and shouted to all of us to step back.

A Frightful Hailstorm
Hailstones Black and Red: Impurity and Pride

We all withdrew a certain distance. From where we stood, we could see the grapes swell up and, though retaining their golden color and oblong shape, become hideous masses resembling shell-less snails. Again the guide shouted: "Watch now: the Lord takes His vengeance." Immediately, the sky darkened and a dense fog covered the vine entirely from our sight. Through the darkness lightning flashed, thunder roared and dreadful thunderbolts struck everywhere over the playground. The vine shoots bent under the furious wind and all the leaves were stripped away. Finally, a hailstorm hit the vine. I tried to flee, but my guide held me back. "Look at the hail," he said.

I noticed that the hailstones, big as eggs, were either black or red, each pointed at one end and flat at the other, like a mallet. Those nearest to me were black, but beyond I could see the red ones.

"It's weird," I exclaimed. "I never saw hailstones like these."

"Get closer," the stranger said, "and you will see something else."

I complied, but an awful stench made me draw back immediately. At the man's insistence, I picked one up to examine it, but, unable to stomach the smell, I dropped it instantly. "I couldn't see anything," I said.

"Try again," he replied.

Overcoming my revulsion, I took up a black hailstone and read on it: "Immodesty."

Then I walked over to the red hailstones. Though ice-cold, they started fires wherever they fell. I picked one up. It still smelled very bad, but I found it easier to read on it: "Pride." Somewhat embarrassed by these findings, I asked: "Are these then the two main vices threatening this house?"

"These are the two main vices that ruin most souls not only in your house but all over the world. In due time, you will see how many will plunge into Hell because of them."

"Then what must I tell my sons to make them abhor them?"

"You will soon find out," he said and moved away from me. Meanwhile, hailstones kept pelting the vine furiously amid thunder and lightning. The grapes were now a mess, looking as if they had been thoroughly crushed by vintners' feet in a vat. The juice fouled the air with such a sickening stench that it was hardly possible to breathe. Each grape gave out a foul smell of its own, each more repelling than the other, depending on the number and kind of sin.

Unable to stand it, I put my handkerchief to my nose and turned to go to my room. I realized then that I was utterly alone. Fr. Francesia, Fr. Rua, Fr. Cagliero and all the others had fled. In that silence and solitude I became so frightened that I broke into a run and woke up.

As you see, this was a very nasty dream, but what happened the following night was much worse. I'll tell you about it soon. What these dreams imply are at present beyond your understanding. I shall explain them in due time. It is late now, and so I will let you go to bed.

We must bear in mind that the grave faults revealed to Don Bosco did not all refer to that specific year, but to future years as well. He not only saw all his past and present Oratory pupils, but countless others, unknown to him, who would attend his schools throughout the world. Similarly, the parable of the fruitless vine in the book of Isaias spans several centuries.

Furthermore, we should not forget for a moment what the guide said: "Not all the boys are now as you see them, but they will be so one day *unless they mend their ways.*" The path of evil leads to the abyss.

We also wish to point out that after the appearance of the vine, a stranger came upon the scene who, though not immediately recognized by Don Bosco, later acted as his guide and interpreter. In narrating these and other dreams, Don Bosco occasionally called him "a stranger" in order to play down what was most striking about his dreams and—let us say it— what too clearly indicated a supernatural intervention.

Taking advantage of the intimacy with which he honored us, we often asked him about this "stranger." Though we did not get a clear-cut answer, we became convinced through other clues that the guide was not always the same. In turn, he may have been an Angel, a deceased pupil, St. Francis de Sales, St. Joseph or some other Saint. On certain occasions, as Don Bosco explicitly stated, Louis Comollo,[1] Dominic Savio and Louis Colle[2] had acted as guides. Sometimes, too, other personages appeared along with them.

---

1. A fellow seminarian of Don Bosco. See Vol. I, pp. 249-256, 329-345.
2. A saintly French youth whom Don Bosco prepared for death in 1881. See Vol. XI, through XVIII.

TO HELL AND BACK   32

(*Biographical Memoirs*, Vol. IX, page 85)

What a frightful and serious meditation is this dream on Hell. Here Don Bosco is illumined from above. Here truth becomes concrete and frees the heart and mind from the chimerical dreams of those who speak lightly of sin and Hell. The Guide points out to Don Bosco a demarcation line beyond which there is no more love, no more friends and no more comfort. Only despair for those who follow the dissolute world.

It is the will of God that we follow Don Bosco in order to save youth. The harvest is immense; more harvesters are needed, harvesters willing to work hard, very hard like Don Bosco our Father, with no mania of reforming Don Bosco's system.

Fidelity is needed.

(Salesians will do well to re-read *Memorie Biografiche*, Vol. XVII, p. 387.)

In this dream about Hell, a clear program is given for the salvation of boys:

"They have their superiors: let them obey them.

"They have rules: let them observe them.

"They have the Sacraments: let them frequent them."

The Salesian system will obtain this through reason, religion and kindness. It requires great bounty and patience. But Mary, Help of Christians will help the educators to crush the head of the malign Serpent and to save youth.

On Sunday night, May 3, 1868, the Feast of St. Joseph's Patronage, Don Bosco resumed the narration of his dreams:

I have another dream to tell you, a sort of aftermath of those I told you last Thursday and Friday which totally exhausted me. Call them dreams or whatever you like. Anyway, as you know, on the night of April 17, a frightful toad seemed bent on devouring me. When it finally vanished, a voice said to me: "Why don't you tell them?" I turned in that direction and saw a distinguished person standing by my bed. Feeling guilty about my silence, I asked: "What should I tell my boys?"

"What you have seen and heard in your last dreams and what you have wanted to know and what you shall have revealed to you tomorrow night!" He then vanished.

I spent the whole next day worrying about the miserable night in store for me, and when evening came, loath to go to bed, I sat at my desk browsing through books until midnight. The mere thought of having more nightmares thoroughly scared me. However, with great effort, I finally went to bed.

Lest I should fall asleep immediately and start dreaming, I set my pillow upright against the headboard and practically sat up, but soon in my exhaustion I simply fell asleep. Immediately the same person of the night before appeared at my bedside. (Don Bosco often called him "the man with the cap.")

"Get up and follow me!" he said.

"For heaven's sake," I protested, "leave me alone. I am exhausted! I've been tormented by a toothache for several days now and need rest. Besides, nightmares have completely worn me out." I said this because this man's apparition always means trouble, fatigue and terror for me.

"Get up," he repeated. "You have no time to lose."

I complied and followed him. "Where are you taking me?" I asked.

"Never mind. You'll see." He led me to a vast, boundless plain, veritably a lifeless desert, with not a soul in sight or a tree or brook. Yellowed, dried-up vegetation added to the desolation. I had no idea where I was or what I was to do. For a moment I even lost sight of my guide and feared that I was lost and utterly alone. Fr. Rua, Fr. Francesia and the others were nowhere to be seen. When I finally saw my friend coming toward me, I sighed in relief.

"Where am I?" I asked.

"Come with me and you will find out!"

"All right. I'll go with you."

He led the way and I followed in silence, but after a long, dismal trudge, I began worrying whether I would ever be able to cross that vast expanse, what with my toothache and swollen legs. Suddenly, I saw a road ahead. "Where to now?" I asked my guide.

"This way," he replied.

The Broad Road

We took the road. It was beautiful, wide and neatly paved. *Via peccantium complanata lapidibus, et in fine illarum inferi, et tenebrae, et poenae*—"The way of sinners is smooth stones and at their end are Hell and darkness and pain." (*Ecclus.* 21:11). Both sides were lined with magnificent verdant hedges dotted with gorgeous flowers. Roses especially peeped everywhere through the leaves. At first glance, the road was level and comfortable, and so I ventured upon it without the least suspicion, but soon I noticed that it insensibly kept sloping downward. Though it did not look steep at all, I found myself moving so swiftly that I felt I was effortlessly gliding through the air. Really, I was gliding and hardly using my feet. Then the thought struck me that the return trip would be very long and arduous.

"How shall we get back to the Oratory?" I asked worriedly.

"Do not worry," he answered. "The Almighty wants you to go. He who leads you on will also know how to lead you back."

The road kept sloping downward. As we were continuing on our way, flanked by banks of roses and other flowers, I became aware that the Oratory boys and very many others whom I did not know were following me. Somehow I found myself in their midst. As I was looking at them, I noticed now one, now another fall to the ground and instantly be dragged by an unseen force toward a frightful drop, distantly visible, which sloped into a furnace. "What makes these boys fall?" I asked my companion. *Funes extenderunt in laqueum; iuxta iter scandalum posuerunt*—"They have spread cords for a net; by the wayside they have laid snares for me." (*Ps.* 139:6).

"Take a closer look," he replied.

I did. Traps were everywhere, some close to the ground, others at eye level, but all well concealed. Unaware of their danger, many boys got caught and tripped; they would sprawl to the ground, legs in the air. Then, when they managed to get back on their feet, they would run headlong down the road toward the abyss. Some got trapped by the head, others by the neck, hand, arms, legs, or sides, and were pulled down instantly. The ground traps, fine as spiders' webs and hardly visible, seemed very flimsy and harmless; yet, to my surprise, every boy they snared fell to the ground.

Noticing my astonishment, the guide remarked: "Do you know what this is?"

"Just some filmy fiber," I answered.

"A mere nothing," he said, "*just plain human respect*."

Seeing that many boys were caught in those traps, I asked: "Why do so many get caught? Who pulls them down?"

"Go nearer and you will see!" he told me.

I followed his advice but saw nothing peculiar.

"Look closer," he insisted.

I picked up one of the traps and tugged. I immediately felt some resistance. I pulled harder, only to feel that, instead of drawing the thread closer, I was being pulled down myself. I did not resist and soon found myself at the mouth of a frightful cave. I halted, unwilling to venture into that deep cavern, and again started pulling the thread toward me. It gave a little, but only through great effort on my part. I kept tugging, and after a long while a huge, hideous monster emerged, clutching a rope to which all those traps were tied together. He was the one who instantly dragged down anyone who got caught in them. "It won't do to match my strength with his," I said to myself. "I'll certainly lose. I'd better fight him with the Sign of the Cross and with short invocations."

Then I went back to my guide. "Now you know who he is," he said to me.

"I surely do! It is the devil himself!"

Knives

Carefully examining many of the traps, I saw that each bore an inscription: Pride, Disobedience, Envy, Sixth Commandment, Theft, Gluttony, Sloth, Anger and so on. Stepping back a bit to see which ones trapped the greater number of boys, I discovered that the most dangerous were those of impurity, disobedience and pride. In fact, these three were linked together. Many other traps also did great harm, but not as much as the first two. Still watching, I noticed many boys running faster than others. "Why such haste?" I asked.

"Because they are dragged by the snare of human respect."

Looking even more closely, I spotted knives among the traps. A providential hand had put them there for cutting oneself free. The bigger ones, symbolizing meditation, were for use against the trap of pride; others, not quite as big, symbolized spiritual reading well made. There were also two swords representing devotion to the Blessed Sacrament—especially through frequent Holy Communion—and to the Blessed Virgin. There was also a hammer symbolizing Confession and other knives signifying devotion to St. Joseph, to St. Aloysius and to other Saints. By these means, quite a few boys were able to free themselves or evade capture.

Indeed I saw some lads walking safely through all those traps, either by good timing before the trap sprung on them or by making it slip off them if they got caught.

Thorns—Arduous Way

When my guide was satisfied that I had observed everything, he made me continue along that rose-hedged road, but the farther we went, the scarcer the roses became. Long thorns began to show up, and soon the roses were no more. The hedges became sun-scorched, leafless and thorn-studded. Withered branches torn from the bushes lay criss-crossed along the roadbed, littering it with thorns and making it impassable. We had come now to a gulch whose steep sides hid what lay beyond. The road, still sloping downward, was becoming ever more horrid, rutted, guttered and bristling with rocks and boulders. I lost track of all my boys, most of whom had left this treacherous road for other paths.

I kept going; but the further I advanced, the more arduous and steep became the descent, so that I tumbled and fell several times, lying prostrate until I could catch my breath. Now and then my guide supported me or helped me to rise. At every step, my joints seemed to give way, and I thought my shinbones would snap. Panting, I said to my guide: "My good fellow, my legs won't carry me another step. I just can't go any farther."

He did not answer, but continued walking. Taking heart, I followed until, seeing me soaked in perspiration and thoroughly exhausted, he led me to a little clearing alongside the road. I sat down, took a deep breath and felt a little better. From my resting place, the road I had already traveled looked very steep, jagged and strewn with loose stones; but what lay ahead seemed so much worse that I closed my eyes in horror.

"Let's go back," I pleaded. "If we go any farther, how shall we ever get back to the Oratory? I will never make it up this slope."

"Now that we have come so far, do you want me to leave you here?" my guide sternly asked.

At this threat, I wailed: "How can I survive without your help?"

"Then follow me."

Enormous Building

We continued our descent, the road now becoming so frightfully steep that it was almost impossible to stand erect. And then, at the bottom of this precipice, at the entrance of a dark valley, an enormous building loomed into sight, its towering portal, tightly locked, facing our road. When I finally got to the bottom, I became smothered by a suffocating heat, while a greasy, green-tinted smoke lit by flashes of scarlet flames rose from behind those enormous walls which loomed higher than mountains.

"Where are we? What is this?" I asked my guide.

"Read the inscription on that portal and you will know."

I looked up and read these words: *Ubi non est redemptio*—"The place of no reprieve." I realized that we were at the gates of Hell. The guide led me all around this horrible place. At regular distances, bronze portals like the first overlooked precipitous descents; on each was an inscription, such as: *Discedite, maledicti, in ignem aeternum qui paratus est diabolo et angelis eius*—"Depart from Me, you cursed into everlasting fire which was prepared for the devil and his angels." (*Matt.* 25:41). *Omnis arbor quae non facit fructum bonum excidetur et in ignem mittetur*—"Every tree that does not bear good fruit is cut down and thrown into the fire." (*Matt.* 7:19).

I tried to copy them into my notebook, but my guide restrained me: "There is no need. You have them all in Holy Scripture. You even have some of them inscribed in your porticoes."

At such a sight I wanted to turn back and return to the Oratory. As a matter of fact, I did start back, but my guide ignored my attempt. After trudging through a steep, never-ending ravine, we again came to the foot of the precipice facing the first portal. Suddenly the guide turned to me. Upset and startled, he motioned to me to step aside. "Look!" he said.

Boys Who Rush Down

I looked up in terror and saw in the distance someone racing down the path at an uncontrollable speed. I kept my eyes on him, trying to identify him, and as he got closer, I recognized him as one of my boys. His disheveled hair was partly standing upright on his head and partly tossed back by the wind. His arms were outstretched as though he were thrashing the water in an attempt to stay afloat. He wanted to stop, but could not. Tripping on the protruding stones, he kept falling even faster. "Let's help him, let's stop him," I shouted, holding out my hands in a vain effort to restrain him.

"Leave him alone," the guide replied.

"Why?"

"Don't you know how terrible God's vengeance is? Do you think you can restrain one who is fleeing from His just wrath?"

Meanwhile, the youth had turned his fiery gaze backward in an attempt to see if God's wrath were still pursuing him. The next moment he fell tumbling to the bottom of the ravine and crashed against the bronze portal as though he could find no better refuge in his flight.

"Why was he looking backward in terror?" I asked.

"Because God's wrath will pierce Hell's gates to reach and torment him even in the midst of fire!"

As the boy crashed into the portal, it sprang open with a roar, and instantly a thousand inner portals opened with a deafening clamor as if struck by a body that had been propelled by an invisible, most violent, irresistible gale. As these bronze doors—one behind the other, though at a considerable distance from each other—remained momentarily open, I saw far into the distance something like furnace jaws spouting fiery balls the moment the youth hurtled into it. As swiftly as they had opened, the portals then clanged shut again. For a third time I tried to jot down the name of that unfortunate lad, but the guide again restrained me. "Wait," he ordered. "Watch!"

Three other boys of ours, screaming in terror and with arms outstretched, were rolling down one behind the other like massive rocks. I recognized them as they too crashed against the portal. In that split second, it sprang open and so did the other thousand. The three lads were sucked into that endless corridor amid a long-drawn, fading, internal echo, and then the portals clanged shut again. At intervals, many other lads came tumbling down after them. I saw one unlucky boy being pushed down the slope by an evil companion. Others fell singly or with others, arm in arm or side by side. Each of them bore the name of his sin on his forehead. I kept calling to them as they hurtled down, but they did not hear me. Again the portals would open thunderously and slam shut with a rumble. Then, dead silence!

The Cause of Many Damnations

"*Bad companions, bad books, and bad habits,*" my guide exclaimed, "are mainly responsible for so many eternally lost."

The traps I had seen earlier were indeed dragging the boys to ruin. Seeing so many going to perdition, I cried out disconsolately: "If so many of our boys end up this way, we are working in vain. How can we prevent such tragedies?"

"This is their present state," my guide replied, "and that is where they would go if they were to die now."

"Then let me jot down their names so that I may warn them and put them back on the path to Heaven."

"Do you really believe that some of them would reform if you were to warn them? Then and there your warning might impress them, but soon they will forget it, saying: 'It was just a dream,' and they will do worse than before. Others, realizing they have been unmasked, will receive the Sacraments, but this will be neither spontaneous nor meritorious; others will go to Confession because of a momentary fear of Hell, but will still be attached to sin."

"Then is there no way to save these unfortunate lads? Please, tell me what I can do for them."

"They have superiors; let them obey them. They have rules; let them observe them. They have the Sacraments; let them receive them."

Just then a new group of boys came hurtling down and the portals momentarily opened. "Let's go in," the guide said to me.

The Entrance into Hell

I pulled back in horror, I could not wait to rush back to the Oratory to warn the boys lest others might be lost as well.

"Come," my guide insisted. "You'll learn much. But first tell me: Do you wish to go alone or with me?" He asked this to make me realize that I was not brave enough and therefore needed his friendly assistance.

"Alone inside that horrible place?" I replied. "How will I ever be able to find my way out without your help?" Then a thought came to my mind and aroused my courage. *Before one is condemned to Hell, I said to myself, he must be judged. And I haven't been judged yet!*

"Let's go," I exclaimed resolutely. We entered that narrow, horrible corridor and whizzed through it with lightning speed. Threatening inscriptions shone eerily over all the inner gateways. The last one opened into a vast, grim courtyard with a large, unbelievably forbidding entrance at the far end. Above it stood this inscription: *Ibunt impii in ignem aeternum*—"And these [the wicked] shall go into everlasting fire." (*Matt.* 25:46). The walls all about were similarly inscribed. I asked my guide if I could read them, and he consented. These were the inscriptions:

Dabo ignem in carnes eorum ut comburantur in semptiernum—"I will give fire . . . into their flesh that they may burn forever." (*Judith* 16:21).

Cruciabuntur die ac nocte in saecula saeculorum—"They will be tormented day and night forever and ever." (*Apoc.* 20:10).

Hic universitas malorum per omnia saecula saeculorum— "Here all kinds of torments forever and ever."

Nullus est hic ordo, sed horror sempiternus inhabitat— "Here disorder and everlasting horror dwell." (*Job* 10:22).

Fumus tormentorum suorum in aeternum ascendit—"The smoke of their torments goes up forever and ever." (*Apoc.* 14:11).

Non est pax impiis—"There is no peace to the wicked." (*Is.* 48:22).

Clamor et stridor dentium—"There shall be weeping and gnashing of teeth." (*Matt.* 8:12).

While I moved from one inscription to another, my guide, who had stood in the center of the courtyard, came up to me.

"From here on," he said, "no one may have a helpful companion, a comforting friend, a loving heart, a compassionate glance, or a benevolent word. All that is gone forever. Do you just want to see or would you rather experience these things yourself?"

"I only want to see!" I answered.

A Narrow Horrible Corridor

"Then come with me," my friend added, and, taking me in tow, he stepped through that gate into a corridor at whose far end stood an observation platform, closed by a huge, single crystal pane reaching from the pavement to the ceiling. As soon as I crossed its threshold, I felt an indescribable terror and dared not take another step. Ahead of me I could see something like an immense cave, which gradually disappeared into recesses sunk far into the bowels of the mountains. They were all ablaze, but theirs was not an earthly fire, with leaping tongues of flames. The entire cave—walls, ceiling, floor, iron, stones, wood and coal—everything was a glowing white at temperatures of thousands of degrees. Yet the fire did not incinerate, did not consume. I simply cannot find words to describe the cavern's horror. *Praeparata est enim ab heri*

Thopeth, a rege praeparata, profunda et dilatata. Nutrimenta eius, ignis et ligna multa; flatus Domini sicut torrens sulphuris succendens eam—"For in Topheth there has been prepared beforehand . . . a pit deep and wide with straw and wood in plenty. The breath of Yahweh, like a stream of brimstone, will set fire to it." (*Is.* 30:33).

I was staring in bewilderment around me when a lad dashed out of a gate. Seemingly unaware of anything else, he emitted a most shrilling scream, like one who is about to fall into a cauldron of liquid bronze, and plummeted into the center of the cave; instantly, he too became incandescent and perfectly motionless, while the echo of his dying wail lingered for an instant more.

Terribly frightened, I stared briefly at him for a while. He seemed to me one of my Oratory boys. "Isn't he so and so?" I asked my guide.

"Yes," was the answer.

"Why is he so still, so incandescent?"

"You chose to see," he replied. "Be satisfied with that. Just keep looking. Besides, *Omnis enim igne salietur et omnis victima sale salietur*—'Everyone shall be salted with fire; every victim shall be salted.'" (*Mark* 9:48).

As I looked again, another boy came hurtling down into the cave at break-neck speed. He too was from the Oratory. As he fell, so he remained. He too emitted one single heartrending shriek that blended with the last echo of the scream that had come from the youth who had preceded him. Other boys kept hurtling in the same way in increasing numbers, all screaming the same way and then all becoming equally motionless and incandescent. I noticed that the first seemed frozen to the spot, one hand and one foot raised into the air; the second boy seemed bent almost double to the floor. Others stood or hung in various other positions, balancing themselves on one foot or hand, sitting or lying on their backs or on their sides, standing or kneeling, hands clutching their hair. Briefly, the scene resembled a large statuary group of youngsters cast into ever more painful postures. Other lads hurtled into that same furnace. Some I knew; others were strangers to me. I then recalled what is written in the Bible to the effect that as one falls into Hell, so he shall forever remain. *Lignum, in quocumque loco ceciderit, ibi erit*—"Where the tree falls, there it shall lie." (*Eccles.* 11:3).

More Boys Fall Down

More frightened than ever, I asked my guide: "When these boys come dashing into this cave, don't they know where they are going?"

"They surely do. They have been warned a thousand times, but they still choose to rush into the fire, because they do not detest sin and are loath to forsake it. Furthermore, they despise and reject God's incessant, merciful invitations to do penance. Thus provoked, Divine Justice harries them, hounds them, and goads them on, so that they cannot halt until they reach this place."

"Oh, how miserable these unfortunate boys must feel in knowing they no longer have any hope," I exclaimed.

"If you really want to know their innermost frenzy and fury, go a little closer," my guide remarked.

I took a few steps forward and saw that many of those poor wretches were savagely striking at each other like mad dogs. Others were clawing their own faces and hands, tearing their own flesh and spitefully throwing it about. Just then the entire ceiling of the cave became as transparent as crystal and revealed a patch of Heaven and their radiant companions safe for all eternity.

God's Mercy Despised

The poor wretches, fuming and panting with envy, burned with rage because they had once ridiculed the just. *Peccator videbit et irascetur; dentibus suis fremet et tabescet*—"The wicked shall see and shall be angry. He shall gnash his teeth and pine away." (*Ps.* 111:10).

"Why do I hear no sound?" I asked my guide.

"Go closer!" he advised.

Pressing my ear to the crystal window, I heard screams and sobs, blasphemies and imprecations against the Saints. It was a tumult of voices and cries, shrill and confused.

"When they recall the happy lot of their good companions," he replied, "they are obliged to admit: *Nos insensati, vitam illorum aestimabamus insaniam et finem illorum sine honore. Ecce quomodo computati sunt inter filios Dei et inter sanctos sors illorum est. Ergo erravimus a via veritatis—*'Fools that we were! Their lives we deemed madness and their deaths dishonored. See how they are accounted among the sons of God; their lot is with the Saints. We, then, have strayed from the way of the truth.'" (*Wis.* 5:4-5).

"That is why they cry out: *Lassati sumus in via iniquitatis et perditionis. Erravimus per vias difficiles, viam autem Domini ignoravimus. Quid nobis profuit superbia? . . . Transierunt omnia illa tamquam umbra—*'We had our fill of the ways of mischief and ruin. We journeyed through impassable deserts, but the way of the Lord we knew not. What did our pride avail us? . . . All those things passed like a shadow.'" (*Wis.* 5:7-9).

"Such are the mournful chants which shall echo here throughout eternity. But their shouts, their efforts and their cries are all in vain. *Omnis dolor irruet super eos!—*'All evil will fall upon them.'" (*Job* 20:22).

"Here time is no more. Here is only eternity."

While I viewed the condition of many of my boys in utter terror, a thought suddenly struck me: "How can these boys be damned?" I asked. "Last night they were still alive at the Oratory!"

"The boys you see here," he answered, "are all dead to God's grace. Were they to die now or persist in their evil ways, they would be damned. But we are wasting time. Let us go on."

Unquenchable Fire

He led me away and we went down through a corridor into a lower cavern, at whose entrance I read: *Vermis eorum non morietur, et ignis non extinguetur*—"Their worm shall not die and their fire shall not be quenched." (*Is.* 66:24). *Dabit Dominus omnipotens ignem et vermes in carnes eorum ut urantur et sentiant usque in sempiternum*—"He will give fire and worms into their flesh, that they may feel for ever." (*Judith* 16:21).

Here one could see how atrocious was the remorse of those who had been pupils in our schools. What a torment was theirs to remember each unforgiven sin and its just punishment, the countless, even extraordinary means they had to mend their ways, persevere in virtue and earn Paradise, and their lack of response to the many favors promised and bestowed by the Virgin Mary. What a torture to think that they could have been saved so easily, yet now are irredeemably lost, and to remember the many good resolutions made and never kept. Hell is indeed paved with good intentions!

In this lower cavern, I again saw those Oratory boys who had fallen into the fiery furnace. Some are listening to me right now; others are former pupils or even strangers to me. I drew closer to them and noticed that they were all covered with worms and vermin, which gnawed at their vitals, hearts, eyes, hands, legs and entire bodies so ferociously as to defy description. Helpless and motionless, they were a prey to every kind of torment. Hoping I might be able to speak with them or to hear something from them, I drew even closer, but no one spoke or even looked at me. I then asked my guide why, and he explained that the damned are totally deprived of freedom. Each must fully endure his own punishment, with absolutely no reprieve whatever.

"And now," he added, "you too must enter that cavern."

"Oh, no!" I objected in terror. "Before going to Hell, one has to be judged. I have not been judged yet, and so I will not go to Hell!"

"Listen," he said, "what would you rather do: visit Hell and save your boys, or stay outside and leave them in agony?"

For a moment I was struck speechless. "Of course, I love my boys and wish to save them all," I replied, "but isn't there some other way out?"

"Yes, there is a way," he went on, "provided you do all you can."

I breathed more easily and instantly said to myself, *I don't mind slaving if I can rescue these beloved sons of mine from such torments.*

"Come inside then," my friend went on, "and see how our good, almighty God lovingly provides a thousand means for guiding your boys to penance and saving them from ever-lasting death."

Taking my hand, he led me into the cave. As I stepped in, I found myself suddenly transported into a magnificent hall whose curtained glass doors concealed more entrances.

Above one of them, I read this inscription: *The Sixth Commandment.* Pointing to it, my guide exclaimed: "Transgressions of this commandment caused the eternal ruin to many boys."

"Didn't they go to Confession?"

"They did, but they either omitted or insufficiently confessed the sins against the beautiful virtue of purity, saying for instance that they had committed such sins two or three times when it was four or five. Other boys may have fallen into that sin but once in their childhood, and, through shame, never confessed it or did so insufficiently. Others were not truly sorry or sincere in their resolve to avoid it in the future. There were even some who, rather than examine their conscience, spent their time trying to figure out how best to deceive their confessor. Anyone dying in this frame of mind chooses to be among the damned, and so he is doomed for all eternity. Only those who die truly repentant shall be eternally happy. Now do you want to see why our merciful God brought you here?" He lifted the curtain and I saw a group of Oratory boys—all known to me—who were there because of this sin. Among them were some whose conduct seems to be good.

"Now you will surely let me take down their names so that I may warn them individually," I exclaimed.

"It won't be necessary!"

"Then what do you suggest I tell them?"

"Always preach against immodesty. A generic warning will suffice. Bear in mind that even if you did admonish them individually, they would promise, but not always in earnest. For a firm resolution, one needs God's grace, which will not be denied to your boys. If they pray, God manifests His love, especially by being merciful and forgiving. On your part, pray and make sacrifices. As for the boys, let them listen to your admonitions and consult their conscience. It will tell them what to do."

We spent the next half hour discussing the requisites of a good Confession. Afterwards, my guide several times exclaimed in a loud voice: *"Avertere! Avertere!"*

"What do you mean?" I asked.

"Change life!"

Attachment to Earthly Things

Perplexed, I bowed my head and made as if to withdraw, but he held me back.

"You haven't seen everything yet," he explained.

He turned and lifted another curtain bearing this inscription: *Qui volunt divites fieri, incidunt in tentationem et laqueum diaboli*—"Those who long to be rich fall a prey to temptation and to the snares of the devil." (*1 Tim.* 6:9).

"This does not apply to my boys," I countered, "because they are as poor as I am. We are not rich and do not want to be. We give it no thought."

As the curtain was lifted, however, I saw a group of boys, all known to me. They were in pain, like those I had seen before. Pointing to them, my guide remarked: "As you see, the inscription does apply to your boys."

"But how?" I asked.

"Well," he said, "some boys are so attached to material possessions that their love of God is lessened. Thus, they sin against charity, piety and meekness. Even the mere desire of riches can corrupt the heart, especially if such a desire leads to injustice. Your boys are poor, but remember that greed and idleness are bad counselors. One of your boys committed substantial thefts in his native town, and though he could make restitution, he gives it not a thought. There are others who try to break into the pantry or the prefect's or economer's office, those who rummage in their companions' trunks for food, money or possessions; those who steal stationery and books . . ."

After naming these boys and others as well, he continued: "Some are here for having stolen clothes, linen, blankets and coats from the Oratory wardrobe in order to send them home to their families; others for willful, serious damage; others yet, for not having given back what they had borrowed or for having kept sums of money they were supposed to hand over to the superior. Now that you know who these boys are," he concluded, "admonish them. Tell them to curb all vain harmful desires, to obey God's law and to safeguard their reputation jealously, lest greed lead them to greater excesses and plunge them into sorrow, death and damnation."

I could not understand why such dreadful punishments should be meted out for infractions that boys thought so little of, but my guide shook me out of my thoughts by saying: "Recall what you were told when you saw those spoiled grapes on the vine." With these words he lifted another curtain which hid many of our Oratory boys, all of whom I recognized instantly. The inscription on the curtain read: *Radix omnium malorum*—"The root of all evils."

"Do you know what that means?" he asked me immediately.

"What sin does that refer to?"

"Pride?"

"No!"

"And yet I have always heard that pride is the root of all evil."

"It is, generally speaking, but, specifically, do you know what led Adam and Eve to commit the first sin for which they were driven away from their earthly paradise?"

"Disobedience?"

"Exactly! Disobedience is the root of all evil."

"What shall I tell my boys about it?"

Obedience

"Listen carefully: the boys you see here are those who prepare such a tragic end for themselves by being disobedient. So-and-so and so-and-so, who you think went to bed, leave the dormitory later in the night to roam about the playground, and, contrary to others, they stray into dangerous areas and up scaffolds, endangering even their lives. Others go to church, but ignoring recommendations, they misbehave; instead of praying, they daydream or cause a disturbance. There are also those who make themselves comfortable so as to doze off during church services, and those who only make believe they are going to church. Woe to those who neglect prayer! He who does not pray, dooms himself to perdition. Some are here because, instead of singing hymns or saying the Little Office of the Blessed Virgin, they read frivolous or—worse yet—forbidden books." He then went on mentioning other serious breaches of discipline.

When he was done, I was deeply moved.

"May I mention all these things to my boys?" I asked, looking at him straight in the eye.

"Yes, you may tell them whatever you remember."

"What advice shall I give them to safeguard them from such a tragedy?"

"Keep telling them that by obeying God, the Church, their parents and their superiors, even in little things, they will be saved."

"Anything else?"

"Warn them against idleness. Because of idleness David

fell into sin. Tell them to keep busy at all times, because the devil will not then have a chance to tempt them."

I bowed my head and promised. Faint with dismay, I could only mutter: "Thanks for having been so good to me. Now, please lead me out of here."

"All right, then, come with me." Encouragingly, he took my hand and held me up because I could hardly stand on my feet. Leaving that hall, in no time at all we retraced our steps through that horrible courtyard and the long corridor. But as soon as we stepped across the last bronze portal, he turned to me and said: "Now that you have seen what others suffer, you too must experience a touch of Hell."

"No, no!" I cried in terror.

Touching the Wall of Hell

He insisted, but I kept refusing.

"Do not be afraid," he told me; "Just try it. Touch this wall."

I could not muster enough courage and tried to get away, but he held me back. "Try it," he insisted. Gripping my arm firmly, he pulled me to the wall. "Only one touch," he commanded, "so that you may say you have both seen and touched the walls of eternal suffering and that you may understand what the last wall must be like if the first is so unendurable. Look at this wall!"

I did intently. It seemed incredibly thick. "There are a thousand walls between this and the real fire of Hell," my guide continued. "A thousand walls encompass it, each a thousand measures thick and equally distant from the next one. Each measure is a thousand miles. This wall therefore is millions and millions of miles from Hell's real fire. It is just a remote rim of Hell itself."

When he said this, I instinctively pulled back, but he seized my hand, forced it open, and pressed it against the first of the thousand walls. The sensation was so utterly excruciating that I leaped back with a scream and found myself sitting up in bed. My hand was stinging and I kept rubbing it to ease the pain. When I got up this morning I noticed that it was swollen. Having my hand pressed against the wall, though only in a dream, felt so real that, later, the skin of my palm peeled off.

Bear in mind that I have tried not to frighten you very much, and so I have not described these things in all their horror as I saw them and as they impressed me. We know that Our Lord always portrayed Hell in symbols because, had He described it as it really is, we would not have understood Him. No mortal can comprehend these things. The Lord knows them and He reveals them to whomever He wills.

The next several nights I could not fall asleep, because I was still upset by this frightful dream. What I told you is but a brief summary of very lengthy dreams. Later I shall talk to you about *human respect, the Sixth and Seventh Commandments and pride.* I shall do nothing more than explain these dreams, which fully accord with Holy Scripture. In fact, they are but a commentary of the Bible's teachings on these matters. Some nights ago I told you something, but I'll tell you the rest and explain it whenever I have a chance to speak to you.

Don Bosco kept his promise. Later, he narrated this dream in a condensed form to the boys of our schools in Mirabello and Lanzo. In the retelling, he introduced variations but made no substantial changes. Likewise, when he spoke of it privately to Salesian priests and clerics, with whom he enjoyed greater familiarity, he would add new particulars. Occasionally, he omitted details when talking to some people, while revealing them to others. Concerning the devil's traps, while discussing bad habits, he elaborated on the devil's tactics for luring victims into Hell. Of many scenes he offered no explanation. For instance, he said nothing about the majestic figures he saw in that magnificent hall, which we are inclined to call "the treasure house of God's mercy for saving boys who would otherwise perish." Were these persons perhaps the principal dispensers of countless graces?

Some variations in his narration stemmed from the multiplicity of simultaneous scenes. As they flashed back into his mind, he would select what he considered most suited to his audience. After all, meditating on the Four Last Things was a habit with him. Such meditation kindled a most lively compassion in his heart for all sinners threatened by such a frightful eternity. This ardent charity helped him overcome any reticence as he prudently but frankly invited even very prominent people to mend their ways. It also made his words so effective as to work many conversions.

(*Biographical Memoirs*, Vol. III, page 25;
page 19 in the English Edition)

The vision took place in 1847, but Don Bosco narrated it only in 1864. We read in the chronicles:

Don Bosco first related it in 1864 when one night, after prayers, as was his custom at times, he gathered the members of his infant congregation in his anteroom for a conference. Among those present were Fr. Victor Alasonatti, Fr. Michael Rua, Fr. John Cagliero,[1] Fr. Celestine Durando and the two clerics John Lazzero and Julius Barberis. After speaking of detachment from the world and from one's own family to follow Our Lord's example, he concluded:

I have already told you of several things I saw as in a dream. From them you can infer how much Our Lady loves and helps us. But now that we are all together alone, I am going to tell you, not just another dream, but something that Our Lady herself graciously showed me. I am doing this that each of us may be convinced that it is Our Lady herself who wants our Congregation. This should spur us to work ever harder for God's greater glory. She wants us to place all our

---

1. John Cagliero entered the Oratory in 1851, was ordained a priest in 1862, later became the first Salesian Bishop, Archbishop and Cardinal. He was the leader of the first missionary expedition to South America (1875). There is a fine biography in two volumes, in Italian, and one in English by Fr. Peter Lappin: *Conquistador,* Salesians, Madras.

trust in her. I am taking you into confidence. Please do not mention what I tell you to anyone else in this house or to outsiders lest you give evil tongues occasion to wag.

One day in 1847, after I had spent much time reflecting on how I might help others, especially the young, the Queen of Heaven appeared to me. She led me into a beautiful garden. There stood there a rustic but wide and charming portico built as a vestibule. Its pillars were dressed with climbing vines whose tendrils, thick with leaves and flowers, stretched upwards together and knitted a graceful awning. The portico opened on a lovely walk that soon became, as far as the eye could see, a breathtakingly beautiful pergola (arbor), whose sides were lined with enchanting roses in full bloom. The ground too was covered with roses. The Blessed Virgin said to me: "Take off your shoes." When I had done so, she added: "Walk under that rose pergola, for this is the path you must take." I gladly removed my shoes, because it would have been a pity to step on such gorgeous roses. I took but a few steps and immediately felt very sharp thorns piercing my feet and making them bleed. I had to stop and turn back.

"I had better wear my shoes," I told my guide. "Yes, indeed," she replied, "sturdy ones." So I put my shoes on again and returned to the rose pergola, followed by a number of helpers who had just showed up and asked to go along with me. They followed me under the indescribably beautiful pergola, but as I went along I noted that it was becoming narrow and low. Many of its branches were draped like festoons; others, instead, just dropped straight down. Some branches, here and there, jutted sideways from the rose stalks, while others formed a thicket which partly blocked the path; still others crept along the ground. All the branches, however, were thick with roses. There were roses around me, roses above me and roses under my feet.

As my feet made me wince with pain, I could not help brushing against the roses at my sides, and even sharper thorns pricked me. But I kept walking. My lacerated legs, though, kept getting entangled in the lower branches. Whenever I

St. John Bosco's dream of the roses and thorns symbolizing the fact that although the path of the Salesians seemed to outsiders "strewn with roses," there were also many thorns underfoot. (Note St. John Bosco's bare feet.)

pushed aside a bough barring my way, or skirted the sides of the pergola to avoid it, the thorns dug into me and made me bleed all over. The roses overhead also were thick with thorns which pricked my head. Notwithstanding, I went forward encouraged by the Blessed Virgin. Now and then, however, some sharper thorns pierced me more than others, and caused greater pain.

Meanwhile, those who were watching me walk under that bower—and they were a crowd—passed comments, such as, "How lucky Don Bosco is! His path is forever strewn with roses. He hasn't a worry in the world. No troubles at all!" But they could not see the thorns that were piercing my poor legs. I called on many priests, clerics[2] and laymen to follow me, and they did so joyfully, enthralled by the beauty of the flowers. When, however, they discovered that they had to walk over sharp thorns and that there was no way to avoid them, they loudly began complaining: "We have been fooled." I answered: "If you are out for a nice time, you had better go back. If not, follow me."

Many turned back. After going on for a while, I turned to look at my followers. You cannot imagine how I felt when I saw that some had disappeared and others had already turned back and were walking away. I went after them and called them back, but it was useless; they would not even listen to me. Then I broke into tears and wept unrestrainedly as I asked myself: "Must I walk this painful path all alone?"

But I was soon comforted. I saw a group of priests, clerics and laymen coming towards me. "Here we are," they said. "We are all yours and ready to follow you." So I led them forward. Only a few lost heart and quit; most of them followed me through.

After walking the whole length of the pergola, I found myself in another enchanting garden, and my few followers gathered around me. They were exhausted, ragged and bleed-

---

2. "Cleric" here means member of the Salesian Society training for the priesthood.

ing, but a cool breeze healed them all. Another gust of wind came and, like magic, I found myself surrounded by a vast crowd of boys, young clerics, coadjutor brothers[3] and even priests who began helping me care for all those boys. Many of these helpers I knew, but many more were strangers.

Meanwhile, I had come to a higher spot in the garden, where a very imposing, majestic building stood. I entered and found myself in a spacious hall so grandiose that I doubt one could find its like in any royal palace. Fresh thornless roses, set all through the hall, filled it with a most delicate fragrance. The Blessed Virgin, who had been my guide all along, now asked me: "Do you grasp the meaning of what you now see and of what you saw before?"

"No," I said. "Please, explain it to me."

She replied: "The path strewn with roses and thorns is an image of your mission among boys. You must wear shoes, a symbol of mortification. The thorns on the ground stand for sensible affections, human likes and dislikes which distract the educator from his true goal, weaken and halt him in his mission and hinder his progress and heavenly harvest. The roses symbolize the burning charity which must be your distinguishing trait and that of your fellow workers. The other thorns stand for obstacles, suffering and disappointments you will experience. But you must not lose heart. Charity and mortification will enable you to overcome all difficulties and lead you to roses without thorns."

As soon as the Mother of God finished speaking, I awoke and found myself in my room.

Don Bosco understood the purport of the dream and concluded by saying that from then on he knew exactly the path he had to follow. Already known to him were the obstacles and snares with which his adversaries would attempt to block his progress. Many would be the thorns on his path, but he was sure, absolutely sure, of God's will in the matter and of

---

3. "Coadjutor brother" here means a lay member of the Salesian Society.

the ultimate success of his great undertaking.

The dream also warned him not to be discouraged by the defection of some who seemed called to help him in his work. Those who first deserted him were priests and laymen who in the early days of the Festive Oratory had volunteered to help him. Those who came later were his own Salesians, and the wind symbolized the forthcoming divine assistance and comfort.

On a later occasion, Don Bosco revealed that this dream, or vision, was repeated in 1848 and 1856, each time under slightly different circumstances, which we have integrated in our narration to avoid repetitions.

Although in 1847 Don Bosco kept this secret to himself, his devotion to the Blessed Virgin became ever more ardent, as we heard from Joseph Buzzetti. Ever more effective were his efforts to urge his boys to keep all the feasts of the Madonna and the month of May for their own spiritual advantage. It was obvious that he had fully entrusted himself to Divine Providence, just as a child throws itself into the arms of its mother. The unhesitating determination he displayed in making decisions when beset by grave problems or difficulties showed clearly enough that he was carrying out a program already laid out for him and that he was taking his guidance from above. It looked as if the directive once given to Moses, "See that you make them according to the pattern shown you," had now been repeated to him. (*Ex.* 25:40).

We might finally add that from time to time various remarks would escape his lips, leading his close associates to believe that there was more than met the eye. On such occasions he seemed to be lovingly gazing on the image of the Blessed Virgin, resplendent on high and inviting all mankind to have recourse to her.

THE
STRUGGLES
OF THE
SOCIETY

34

(*Biographical Memoirs*, Vol. XIV, p. 123)

A prophetic dream was narrated by Don Bosco on May 9, 1879. In it he saw the relentless fights that would have to be faced by *those who are called to the Salesian Congregation*, and he received a series of useful advices for all and some salutary instructions for the future.

There was first a fierce and long fight between some boys and warriors of diverse aspects, diverse shapes, with strange weapons. At the end there were very few survivors.

Then another more fierce and horrible battle took place between monsters of gigantic size and men of high stature, well armed and well trained. They carried a very high and very broad banner, in the center of which were painted in gold these words: *MARIA AUXILIUM CHRISTIANORUM*—"Mary, Help of Christians." The battle was long and bloody. But those who followed the banner were invulnerable and remained masters of a very vast plain.

Those lads who had survived the previous battle joined these, and all together they formed a sort of army, each one carrying as a weapon in the right hand the holy crucifix and in the left hand a small banner of Mary, Help of Christians, similar to the one mentioned above.

The new soldiers performed many maneuvers in that vast plain; then they separated, and some left for the East, a few for the North and many for the South.

These having disappeared, there were renewed again the same battles, the same maneuvers and departures for the same directions.

I recognized some soldiers from the first battles: those that followed afterwards were unknown to me, but they showed that they knew me, and asked me many questions.

Soon after there followed a downpour of shining little flames of fire of various colors. It thundered, and then the sky cleared up and I found myself in a most delightful garden. A man who looked like St. Francis de Sales offered me a booklet without saying a word. I asked who he was. "Read in the book," he answered.

I opened the book, but was hardly able to read it. I could, however, make out these precise words:

To the Novices: Obedience in everything. Through obedience they will merit the blessing of the Lord and the good will of men. Through diligence they will combat and conquer the snares of their spiritual enemies.

To the Professed: To guard jealously the virtue of chastity. To love the good name of the Confreres and to promote the decorum of the Congregation.

To the Directors: Every care, every fatigue in order to observe and make others observe the Rules through which everyone has consecrated himself to God.

To the Superior: Absolute holocaust in order to win over himself and his subjects for God.

Many other things were printed in that book, but I was not able to read more, because paper and ink appeared blue.

"Who are you?" again I asked that man who was looking at me with a serene countenance.

"My name is known to all the good people, and I have been sent to communicate to you some future events."

"Which?"

"Those already shown and those which you will ask."

"What must I do to promote vocations?"

"The Salesians will have many vocations through their virtuous conduct, treating their pupils with the greatest charity and insisting on frequent Communion."

"What ought to be observed in accepting novices?"

"One ought to exclude the lazy and the gluttonous."

"In admitting to the vows?"

"To watch if there be a guarantee of chastity."

"How can good spirit in our houses be best preserved?"

"By writing, by visiting, by receiving, and by treating with benevolence; and this with great frequency on the part of the Superiors."

"And what about our conduct concerning the Missions?

"Only persons who are sure regarding morality can be sent there; should anyone be seriously suspected he ought to be recalled; to study how to cultivate indigenous vocations.

"Does our Congregation go on well?"

"*Qui justus est justificetur adhuc. Non progredi est regredi. Qui perseveraverit salvus erit*"—"He that is just, let him be justified still. There is no progressing and regressing. He who will persevere will be saved."

"Will it expand much?"

"As long as the Superiors will do their part, it will advance, and nobody will be able to arrest its progress."

"Will it last long?"

"Your Congregation will last as long as the members will love *work* and *temperance*. Failing one of these pillars, your edifice will tumble down, crushing Superiors and inferiors and their followers."

At this moment there appeared four men carrying a coffin. They came walking towards me.

"For whom is this?" I asked.

"For you."

"Soon?"

"Do not ask about this: only remember that you are mortal."

"What do you mean by this coffin?"

"That whatever you want your sons to practice after you, you must make them practice while you live. This is the inheritance, the testament which you ought to leave to your sons. But you must prepare it and leave it completed and well practiced."

"What is in store for us, flowers or thorns?"

"Many roses are in store, many consolations, but imminent are very sharp thorns that will cause to all profound bitterness and anguish. Much prayer is wanted!"

"Must we go to Rome (to found houses)?"

"Yes, but slowly, with the greatest prudence and with studied caution."

"Is the end of my mortal life near?"

"Do not worry about this. You have the Rules, you have books; do whatever you teach others. Watch!"

I wanted to ask more questions, but I heard a loud burst of thunder with lightnings and thunderbolts, while some men, or rather horrid monsters, rushed upon me to tear me to pieces. At that moment a gloomy darkness hid everything from my sight. I thought my end had come, and I began to scream frantically. Then I woke up and found I was still alive, and it was 4:45 in the morning.

If there is anything that can be profitable for us, let us accept it. And in all things, honor and glory be to God forever and ever.

THE PHYLLOXERA **35**

A dream-vision on murmuring and disobedience, and the remedy to be applied. A
warning. (*Biographical Memoirs*, Vol. XII,
page 475)

First Week of October 1876

The following dream was told by Don Bosco at the end of
the third retreat held at Lanzo during the vacations of 1876,
from the 1st to the 7th of October, and in the chronicles is
recorded as follows:

Don Bosco saw himself in an immense hall. Religious from
various Orders were gathered there in great numbers. Upon
his arrival, all eyes were turned toward him as though he had
been expected. He saw, too, among the crowd a man in a
very strange garb: his head was wrapped in a white kerchief,
and his body was cloaked in a sort of white sheet. He enquired
who that "mad-cap" could be; and he was told that "that funny
fellow" was himself—Don Bosco, the dreamer!

He advanced among that multitude of religious, who made
a great smiling circle around him, without speaking a word.
He looked around at them in great surprise, but all continued to look at him, laughing and in silence. Finally, he spoke
himself:

"Why do you laugh at me so?" he said. "Are you having
a joke at my expense?"

"Not at all," some answered. "We are only laughing because
we know the motive that brought you here."

"How do you know that, since I am not certain of it myself? To be sure, your laughing surprises me."

"The motive is that you have just given the retreat to your clerics at Lanzo."

"And what for that?"

"Now you have come to find out what to tell them in your concluding address."

"Let it be so, then! and I beg you to oblige me; I want some good advice for them, which may help to prosper the Congregation of St. Francis de Sales ever more. Can you give it to me?"

"We will make only one suggestion: *Tell your children to guard themselves against the 'phylloxera.'*"

"The phylloxera? What has this to do with my Congregation?"

"*If you manage to keep the phylloxera from your Congregation, it will have a long life, and it will flourish and do much good to countless souls.*"

"I don't understand you."

"Don't you? The scourge of the phylloxera has ruined many a religious Order, and it is preventing many others from attaining to their noble ends."

"I beg your pardon, but your advice will be useless to me unless you explain it. I can make nothing of it."

"Then it wasn't worth your while to study so much theology."

"I hope I have done my duty at that, but I never came across a treatise which mentions the phylloxera."

"Neverthless, theology says much about the phylloxera. What is the moral and spiritual sense of this word?"

"I fail to see even a distant hint at any spiritual application in the etymological root of the word."

"Since you can't read into this mystery, here comes one who will explain it to you."

At this moment, Don Bosco perceived a certain movement in the crowd; a passage was being opened for someone. Presently, a newcomer appeared and advanced between the lines toward him. Don Bosco scanned his features, but he seemed a perfect stranger to him, though his familiar manner was that of an old acquaintance. He at once addressed the stranger:

"You are welcome, if you get me out of this tangle in which these gentlemen have placed me. They want me to believe that the phylloxera is threatening the destruction of religious houses, and they want me to take the phylloxera as the subject matter of the last talk of the retreat."

"Does Don Bosco think himself a wise man?" he replied, "while he does not know these things? *It is most certain that if you will fight the phylloxera might and main, and will get your children to do the same, your society will never fail to flourish.* Do you know what the scourge of the phylloxera is?"

"I know it is a disease which attacks plants and trees and causes great harm."

"What do you think is the cause of the disease?"

"An infinite multitude of tiny germs which set on a plant and take complete possession of it."

"How can you save the neighboring plants from this pest?"

"This I don't know."

"Mind well what I am telling you. The phylloxera appears first on one plant or tree, and it is not long before the neighboring ones are attacked, even if they are at a certain distance. When the pest appears in a vineyard, orchard or garden, it spreads very rapidly; and all the beauty and the hope of fruit is brought to naught. Do you know how it spreads? Not by contact, because distance prevents it, not by creeping from tree to tree, for this has been proved by experiment; *it is the wind that carries the phylloxera from one unit to another*; and thus the whole hillside or the smiling plain is quickly laid waste. In like manner the wind of murmuring, of backbiting, carries abroad the phylloxera of disobedience. Do you understand?"

"Now I begin to understand."

"The harm this kind of phylloxera is doing when spread

by such wind is beyond reckoning. It first COOLS MUTUAL CHARITY even in the most flourishing houses; the ZEAL for the salvation of souls burns low; next, IDLENESS is rampant; finally, all religious VIRTUES disappear, and public SCANDAL makes of what was first revered and admired an object of the REPROBATION of God and men. Neither is it necessary that an infected member should pass from one house to another for the pest to spread. The wind of tale-bearing is sufficient to do the fatal work. Believe me and be convinced, this was the cause of the downfall of certain religious Orders."

"I recognize the truth of your words. But how can such a great misfortune be prevented?"

"Half measures won't help; extreme remedies must be employed. Many means have been tried to exterminate the phylloxera, but in vain. Cutting down and burning is the only effective means. And this must be done promptly, at the very first appearance of any sign of it. The infected tree must be burned immediately with all that is around it in order to save the vineyard. If the whole vineyard is infected, then the whole of it must be brought to ashes, for the sake of the neighboring vineyards. Therefore, *when the phylloxera of the opposition to the will of the Superiors, of proud negligence of the Rule, of contempt for the duties of common life*, make their appearance in a house, then you must not delay: root up that house from its foundations, turn away its members, do not be overcome by a pernicious tolerance. And as you deal with a house, so deal with any individual. At times it may seem that if a member is isolated, he will be cured and will do good again; or perhaps you would not like to expose him, because of your great affection for him, or because of his high attainments and ability, which could enhance the good name of the Congregation; let no such reflections influence you. These persons hardly ever change habits. I will not say their conversion is impossible, but I maintain that it happens very seldom; so seldom in fact that its possibility is no sufficient motive for a Superior to adopt the more lenient course. Certain people, it may be objected, will do worse out in the world. That is their own concern; *they will bear the consequences of their own pride; but your Congregation will be safe from harm.*"

"What if by retaining them in the Society, they could really be brought back to the good path by means of great patience?"

"This is a vain supposition. It is better to dismiss a proud subject of this kind than to retain him with a doubt that he might continue to sow cockle in the vineyard of the Lord. Keep this maxim well in mind; in case of need put it firmly into practice. Make it a matter for special talks to your Directors, and let this be the subject of your closing address of the retreat."

"I thank you very much for your kind advice. With the help of God I will do my best to carry it out. But, please, now tell me who you are."

"Don't you know me anymore? Don't you remember how often we have met and talked together?"

While the stranger spoke thus to him, the bystanders smiled.

At this moment the rising bell rang, and Don Bosco woke up.

THE BULL, THE CARRIAGES AND THE NAILS

36

(*Biographical Memoirs*, Vol. XII, p. 463)

At one of the spiritual retreats held at Lanzo (Turin) in the month of September 1876, there were about 250 retreatants: they were Salesians, novices and aspirants. At the end of the retreat, Don Bosco had the pleasure of receiving thirty-six religious professions (eighteen made temporary vows and eighteen perpetual vows).

As a souvenir of the retreat, Don Bosco narrated a symbolic dream—one of the most instructive he had had till then.

Fr. Lemoyne made notes while Don Bosco was speaking; then he wrote it out more at length and showed it to Don Bosco, who made some slight changes on Don Lemoyne's manuscript.

For clarity, we divide the narration into four parts.

Part I: The Roaring Bull and Humility

We are often told not to bother about our dreams: to tell you frankly, I am of the same opinion in the greater number of cases. Yet, at times, even though these dreams do not reveal the future to us, they certainly help us to solve many knotty problems and teach us to act with true prudence in our varied undertakings. In such case, I think, one may draw from these dreams whatever one finds good and useful.

I would like to tell you just now a dream that has been

haunting me during the whole of this spiritual retreat and particularly last night. I shall narrate it to you exactly as I dreamed it, only condensing some parts here and there, lest I should be too long, because I know that this dream is rife with many wholesome teachings.

It seemed to me that all of us were going together from Lanzo to Turin. We were traveling by some vehicle; I could not tell you whether it was the train or the coach, but I am sure we were not going on foot. After a while, I do not remember on what spot of the road, our conveyance came to a standstill. Eager to learn the cause of this unexpected halt, I got down from the carriage, only to meet the gaze of an eminent person, whom, I fear, I cannot adequately describe. He seemed to be both tall and short at the same time; both fat and lean; though white of complexion, he was also red; he trod the earth and yet walked in the air. I was beside myself with astonishment and, though at a loss to explain this phenomenon, I plucked up courage and boldly asked:

"Who are you?"

Without paying heed to my question, he answered: "Come."

I was bent on knowing first who he was and what he wanted, but he continued, "Come, quickly: let us turn the conveyance into this field." The strange thing about him was that he spoke both loud and soft at the same time and in different voices. This kept me marveling for a very long time.

The field was immense and to all appearances quite flat. There was not a furrow in it, but everything was beaten down flat as a threshing floor. We did not know what to say and, seeing the personage so resolute in his commands, we turned the vehicle into that vast field and ordered everyone down. In the twinkling of an eye, the whole group got down, and to our surprise, the vehicle vanished from our sight. "Now that we have alighted, you will tell me . . . your honor will be so kind as to let me know . . . Your Excellency will condescend to inform me why you have stopped us in this strange place," I muttered, not knowing how to conduct myself in the presence of this august personage. To this he replied: "For a very weighty reason; it is because I want to avert a great danger from you."

"What danger?" I inquired.

"The danger lies in an infuriated bull that kills any person it meets. *Taurus rugiens quaerens quem devoret*," said that individual. "A roaring bull seeking whom he may devour."

"But, my dear man, you apply to the bull what St. Peter in Holy Scripture applies to the lion: *leo rugiens*," I rejoined.

"That does not matter in the least; there it was *leo rugiens*, and here it is *taurus rugiens*. What matters is to be on the alert. Call your followers to your side. Warn them carefully and ask them to lie flat with their faces to the earth as soon as they hear the deafening roar of the bull, and to remain in such a position until the bull has gone by. Woe to the one that does not pay heed to your voice. He who does not lie with his face to the ground shall be lost; for we read in the Holy Scripture that *"he who humbleth himself shall be exalted, and he that exalteth himself shall be humbled: qui se humiliat exaltabitur et qui se exalt humiliabitur."*

Then he added: "Quick, quick, the bull is about to come; shout, shout at the top of your voice and bid all lower themselves." I yelled out, and he kept on saying: "Keep it up! Take courage and cry out even louder; shout, shout!"

I shouted myself hoarse, and I am afraid I even woke up Fr. Lemoyne who was sleeping in the adjacent room; I was not capable of doing more.

After a moment we heard the distant bellow of the bull, whereupon that personage began: "Look out! Look out! Arrange them in two lines close to one another, with a space in between for the bull to pass through."

I shouted out the required orders; in a split second all were lying flat with their face to the ground; from the hazy horizon we noticed the wild bull rapidly advancing; although the majority of us had fallen on our faces, a few, led by curiosity, wanted to see what sort of thing this bull was, and so they refused to follow our example.

That personage then turned to me and said: "Now you will

see what is going to befall these individuals; you will see what they will receive for not obeying orders, not humbling themselves."

I wished at all costs to warn them once again, to shout out to them and to run to their aid; but that personage forbade me to do so. Once again I insisted on approaching them; whereupon he addressed me in a commanding tone. "You too are bound to obedience; down, fall on your face immediately!"

I had hardly stretched myself on the field when a deafening and frightful bellow was heard. The bull was near. All of us trembled and some kept anxiously asking: "What's going to happen next? We are lost!" "Fear not; lie flat," I shouted back. In the meantime, that personage kept on repeating these words: "*Qui se humiliat exaltabitur, et qui se exaltat humiliabitur . . . qui se humiliat . . . qui se humiliat . . .*" Something very strange made me marvel very much. It was this: that although I lay flat on the ground with my very eyes in the dust, yet I was able to see very well the things that took place around me. The bull had seven horns almost in the form of a circle. There were two beneath its nostrils; two in the place of its eyes; two in the usual place and one above these. But behold the wonder! These horns were very strong, movable to right or left or forward at the command of the beast, in such a manner that all it had to do to hurl a person down was to move ahead without turning its head to strike its victim. The horns beneath the nostrils of the brute were the longest and the ones which caused the heaviest slaughter.

Now the animal was very near us. My guide then shouted: "We shall witness the effect of humility."

In an instant, to our great surprise, we were lifted up into the air to a considerable height, to where the raging bull would never have been able to reach. Those who had not lowered themselves to the ground did not enjoy this privilege. The bull made for them straight away and tore them to pieces. Not one was spared. We, on the other hand, who had been raised into the air, feared very much and remarked: "If we fall down now, we are lost! What an unhappy lot is ours!

Who knows what's going to happen to us?!"

The raging bull, after claiming its first victims, tried to get at us; it leapt into the air trying to strike us. But all to no avail. Irritated by its failure, it determined to go away in search of other bulls and seemed to say: *"Then together we shall scale up there . . ."* and so saying, it departed, *habens iram magnam*—"filled with great wrath."

Then we came back to earth; that mysterious personage raised his voice and cried out: "Let us turn towards the south."

Part II: The Savage Bulls and the Blessed Sacrament

And lo! a new scene before us! In turning our eyes toward the south, our troubled gaze met the Blessed Sacrament. The field had disappeared, and we felt that we were in a huge church, artistically decorated, with an altar all alive with burning candles. While we were immersed in profound adoration before the Blessed Sacrament, many savage bulls with horrible horns appeared on the scene, attempting in vain to fall on us. But they could do us no harm, because we were in prayer before the Blessed Sacrament. We immediately began the recitation of the chaplet in honor of the Sacred Heart of Jesus. After a short while, we turned round only to find that the bulls had left. We turned round again towards where the altar had stood, and lo! the candles had disappeared, the Blessed Sacrament was no longer exposed; the church too had disappeared. "But where are we?" we inquired of one another.

We were once again in our old field.

By now you must have understood that the bull represents the devil, the enemy of our soul, who bears us a great hatred and is continually trying to do us harm. The seven horns are the seven capital sins. The only way of escaping the horns of this beast, that is, the assaults of the devil, is the practice of humility, the foundation of all virtues, and the Holy Eucharist, the Bread of the strong.

Part III: The Future Successes of the Salesian Congregation and Conditions for Their Attainment

Astonished at such prodigies, we kept looking at one another; no one dared speak; we did not know what to say. Everyone expected Don Bosco or the august personage to say something. At this juncture my mysterious guide drew near me and whispered in my ear: "Come, I shall show you the triumph that awaits the Society of St. Francis de Sales. Climb that rock and see for yourself!"

I scaled up that huge boulder, the only one in that unbroken plain. What a grandiose spectacle met my gaze! That field, which did not seem very big at first, now appeared to be as large as the whole earth! In there, I saw men of all colors, in every kind of dress and from every nation. I do not know if the earth is capable of holding the number of persons I saw in that plain. I stopped to observe more closely the ones nearest to me. They were dressed like ourselves. I recognized those in the first lines, among whom were many Salesians who were leading troops of boys and girls. Others followed up with other troops, and yet others and others whom I did not know nor could make out, for they were very many. Towards the south I saw Sicilians, Africans and interminable ranks of people whom I did not know. These people were always guided by Salesians. I knew only those in the front ranks. Those in the rear were totally unknown to me.

"Turn around," commanded my guide. Another endless multitude of people caught my eye. Their dress differed from ours; they wore furs in the shape of mantles, which from a distance looked like velvet of different colors. I was then asked to turn to the four cardinal points; among the many other things that I saw in the East were women with very small feet, who struggled very hard to stand and found it a hard task to walk. The particular feature of this sight was that Salesians everywhere were leading groups of boys and girls, and together with them a large number of other people. I recognized those Salesians only who were in the front ranks;

those who followed were unknown to me. I did not even recognize my missionaries. I cannot give you any further details, because, I am afraid, my narration would be too long.

The personage, who till now had acted as my guide, said: "Look and ponder over this! You may not understand now all that I tell you, but mind it well. All this that you have seen is the great harvest that awaits the Salesians. Do you not see its greatness? This immense field in which you stand is the one wherein the Salesians will have to work. The Salesians whom you see before you are the laborers in this vineyard of the Lord. Many are working indeed, and you recognize them, but as the horizon widens out, you gaze on people whom you don't know; this is to tell you that not only will the Salesians work in their field during this century (1876-1900), but also in the next one (1900-2000), and in those yet to come. But do you know what is required in order to realize this? I shall tell; mark my words. Look here: *get these words printed and let them serve as your motto,* as your password, the coat-of-arms of your Congregation. Take note of them: WORK AND TEMPERANCE ALONE WILL CAUSE THE SALESIAN CONGREGATION TO FLOURISH. These words should be *explained, repeated* and *insisted upon* by you. You should print a manual wherein you should fully explain this, and make your followers understand that *'Work and temperance' is your bequest to the Congregation and at the same time its glory.'*

I eagerly added: "This will I do most willingly; in fact this has been our aim so far. It is exactly this that I am continually recommending. I never fail to insist upon this whenever an occasion comes."

"So then are you quite convinced of this?" asked my guide. "Have you perfectly understood me? This you shall bequeath to your children as a patrimony, but tell them plainly that as long as they shall live up to this motto they shall always have followers from the North, the South, the East and the West. Now bring the retreat to a close and send your children to their field of labor. These sons of yours will serve as models for those who will come later on."

He had hardly finished speaking when some vehicles appeared on the scene to take us away to Turin. I kept straining my eyes to see what kind of vehicles they were. They were constructed in a very strange way; the only ones of their kind I had ever seen. Those who were with me immediately climbed up into the conveyance; I was a bit preoccupied about their safety, for those vehicles were without boards at the sides, and so I was not inclined to let them depart. But the personage turned to me and said: "Let them leave! They do not need any protection, provided they practice well the following advice: *SOBRII ESTOTE et VIGILATE*—'Be sober and be watchful.' If this is practiced to the letter, I can assure you that no one will fall down, even though the carriage has no protecting boards."

Part IV: Evils To Be Guarded Against in Order to Ensure the Prosperity of the Congregation

I was now alone with that august personage. "Come," he added promptly, "come; I have still to show you the most important thing; you will have much to learn from that. Do you see that carriage in the distance?"

"I do," I replied.

"Do you know what it is?" he asked.

"I am sorry, I cannot make it out well enough."

"Get closer, if you wish to see it better," he continued. "Do you see that placard? Get closer and observe it minutely; thereon is stamped its coat-of-arms, from which you will be able to know it."

I drew nearer and only found that the placard bore the painting of *four huge nails*. Turning to my guide, I said: "I shall never be able to understand, unless you explain this to me." To this he replied:

"Do you not see those four nails? Look at them closely. They are the four nails that pierced and cruelly tormented our Divine Saviour."

"What has that to do with us?" I anxiously rejoined. Whereupon he continued:

"They are the *four nails that torment the Religious Congregations.* If you succeed in avoiding these four nails, namely, if your Congregation is not tormented by them, and you know how to ward them off, then rest assured that things will go well, and you will be safe."

"But I am no wiser than before," I complained. "What do these nails symbolize?"

"You will understand better if you inspect this carriage which bears the four nails as its emblem. Note also that the carriage has *four compartments,* each one of which corresponds to a particular nail."

"What do these compartments mean?" I asked.

"Come and look at the first one."

I drew nearer and read on the placard: *QUORUM DEUS VENTER EST*—"Those whose god is their stomach." "Now I begin to understand something," I said.

My guide then began to explain things to me. "This is the first nail that torments and ruins many religious Congregations. This will play havoc with yours also, if you are not on the lookout. Fight this enemy sternly, and you may be sure that things will go well with you."

We moved on to the second compartment and I read these words above the second nail: *QUAERUNT QUAE SUA SUNT NON QUAE JESU CHRISTI*—"They seek the things that are their own and not the things of Jesus Christ." "Here are those," he said gravely, "who seek an easy life with all its comforts, and who work for their own good or for their parents, to the detriment of the Society for which they really ought to labor as the portion of Jesus Christ. Watch! By keeping this scourge at a distance, you shall witness the growth of the Congregation."

We then turned to the third compartment. This is what I read near the third nail: *ASPIDIS LINGUA EORUM*—"A viper's is their tongue." The personage proceeded to explain calmly: "Those who murmur and backbite pierce the Congregation with a fatal nail. They are ill at ease until they have given vent to their criticism, right or wrong."

CUBICULUM OTIOSITATIS—"Chamber of laziness" is what I read on the fourth compartment. The mysterious personage continued with his warning. "Here we meet a great number of idlers. When the devil of idleness gains a footing in a religious house, that Community is well nigh to total ruin. On the other hand, as long as you work hard and very much, you may be sure that no such danger will befall you. Now note another thing in the carriage, which is very often overlooked and to which I wish you to pay particular attention. Do you see that space there, which does not form part of any compartment and yet extends to all, being in the center?"

"Yes, I see it," I replied; "but there is nothing besides bits of dried leaves, tall weeds and entangled grass of different lengths."

"Good, this is exactly what I wanted to point out to you," he added.

"But how is this going to be useful to me?" I eagerly asked him.

"Read attentively these words which lie hidden here."

I did as I was commanded, and I read: *LATET ANGUIS IN HERBA*—"There hides a snake in the grass."

"What does this mean?" I curiously inquired. And he explained: "Be on your guard, because there are some who try to hide themselves; they hardly speak at all; they never open their hearts to their Superiors; beware! *Latet anguis in herba*. They are a scourge, a real plague to the Congregation. The bad ones stand a chance of being corrected when they reveal themselves; but these are completely hidden. Nobody notices this; but the evil gathers force, the poison increases in the hearts of these unfortunate ones, and if we shall come to know them at all, it is always too late when the havoc caused is already irreparable . . . Get acquainted with those things which you must keep far away from the Congregation; keep fixed in your mind all that you have heard; enjoin on your followers the duty of explaining and re-explaining at length all these things. If you follow this advice, you need not be anxious about the future of your Congregation, because things will be going better from day to day.

Thereupon I begged my guide to allow me some time to jot down a few notes lest I should forget something. But he curtly replied: "You may try to do it, but I am afraid you will not have time; and now be on your guard!"

I had set myself to write when I heard a confused rumbling sound in the distance which rapidly drew nearer. The whole field seemed to tremble under the shock. Anxious to know if anything new was happening, I turned around, only to find my boys who had left me a short while ago returning frightened; close behind them was the bellowing bull. The sight of the bull for the second time frightened me so much that I woke up with a start.

I have chosen to narrate this dream to you on the eve of our separation, because I am convinced it will bring the retreat to a happy close if we resolve to live up to our motto: WORK and TEMPERANCE; and if we try to work with might and main to avoid the four big nails that mark the death-warrant of religious Societies: the *vice of gluttony, seeking one's comforts, murmuring* and *idleness*. Let me remind you to be always frank, crystal-clear and confident with your Superiors. With this as our rule of life, we shall do a world of good first to our souls and then to those whom Divine Providence will send to us!"

Don Bosco had originally planned, and then promised in the course of his talk, to explain later at length the point on temperance by narrating an appendix to the dream. But when he began the second part of the discourse, it must have completely escaped him. When he was awakened so rudely by the appearance of the infuriated bull, he still desired to know something more and he was granted this when he fell asleep again. Don Bosco narrated the remaining part of this dream at Chieri, and Don Berto, who heard it, sent a copy of it to Don Lemoyne.

I was anxious to *see the effects of temperance and intemperance,* and with this thought uppermost in my mind, I lay to rest. I had hardly fallen asleep when the personage appeared and invited me to follow him to see the effects of temperance. I was led into a delightful garden, full of beautiful flowers of every kind; it was a gorgeous display. Marvelous roses, the symbol of charity, were there in profusion, carnations, jasmines, lilies, violets, evergreens, sunflowers and an infinite variety of other flowers, each symbolizing some virtue.

"Look out!" cried my guide. Almost immediately, the garden disappeared and there followed a deep rumbling noise.

"What's all this? Whence this noise?" I inquired.

"Cast your glance behind and see for yourself."

I obeyed promptly and lo! what a queer spectacle! I saw a large cart, box-like in shape, drawn by a pig and a toad of enormous size. "Draw near and look in," commanded the personage.

I advanced to examine closely the contents of the carriage: it was full to the top with most loathsome animals: crows, serpents, scorpions, basilisks, snails, bats, crocodiles and salamanders, all slimy and most repulsive. I could no longer face such a sight; the nauseous stench that arose from those beasts forced me to turn aside. This abrupt turning away woke me up with a start, but the stench in my nostrils persisted for yet a long time. The impression caused by that horrid sight on my mind was sufficient to keep me awake for the remaining part of the night.

N.B. Evidently, the flowers of the "Delightful Garden" symbolize the virtues which blossom in the nursery of temperance, and the repulsive animals of the cart represent the vices which spring from intemperance.

For further readings on *temperance,* one can consult the analytical index of the *Biographical Memoirs,* under the word "Temperance."

Salesians may study Fr. Favini's book *Alle fonti della Vita Salesiana,* pages 139-162, as a commentary on the above dream.

THE FIRST MISSIONARY DREAM (1872) 37

(*Biographical Memoirs*, Vol. X, page 53)

When negotiations started between the government of Argentina and Don Bosco for a missionary expedition, the meaning of a certain dream, or vision, which he had had years before, began to be clear to the mind of Don Bosco. This is how Don Bosco narrated it:

I found myself suddenly transported into some wild and unknown region. The whole country formed an immense, uncultivated plain, whose flatness was unrelieved by either hill or mountain. I saw there in that plain, immense crowds of men running hither and thither, men of ferocious aspect and of extraordinary stature, with bronzed, almost black complexions and long, stiff hair. Their only garments were animal skins, which they wore hanging from the shoulders, and for weapons each one carried a rude spear and sling.

These groups of men, scattered over the plain, seemed to be engaged in various occupations. Some were hunting wild animals, others were marching along brandishing large pieces of bloody flesh on the points of their spears; some of the groups were engaged in pitched battles amongst themselves; others had fallen into the hands of a company of soldiers in European dress. The ground all around was strewn with dead and dying men.

I stood aghast at this horrifying spectacle, and then, suddenly, from one end of the plain, there appeared a number of persons who were, as I guessed from their dress and way of acting, missionaries belonging to various Orders of the Church, who drew near to preach the true religion of Christ. As they passed along, I scrutinized them very closely, but I did not recognize any of them. Fearlessly, they walked into the midst of the savages, but these, at the sight of them, seemed to be thrown into a diabolical fury. They fell upon them, slew and quartered them, and impaled large pieces of their still warm flesh on the points of their spears. After this, the former scenes were renewed—continual civil war and war with neighboring peoples!

After witnessing so many scenes of horror and bloodshed, I said to myself: "How can a people so brutal and ferocious ever be converted to the true Faith?" Almost immediately, in answer to my thought, I beheld away in the distance another band of missionaries who drew nearer and nearer to the savages. These newcomers were gay and joyful in their bearing, and were *preceded by a large crowd of lively and cheerful boys*.

I looked on with fear and trembling, for I felt certain that they were coming to sure death. I drew nearer and looked attentively at them and recognized in that missionary band our own Salesians. Those in front I knew quite well, not those who followed; but I recognized that they were all Salesians.

"How has this come about?" I asked myself; and I wanted to cry out to them to stop from approaching further. I expected at every moment to see them meet with the same fate that had befallen the former missionaries; but what was my surprise to see that, on their beholding them, a wave of joyful enthusiasm seemed to penetrate through all those savage tribes! They threw down their spears, changed their ferocious aspect, and went to receive the missionaries with every sign of esteem and contentment.

Astonished at this sudden change, I was curious to see how it would all end. Looking attentively, I saw how the missionaries were instructing and teaching the natives, who listened to them with great attention and interest. I saw how quick to learn they were, and how readily they sought at once to put it into practice.

I watched on and observed that the missionaries began to *recite the Rosary*, and that the savages ran from every direction to take part in this prayer.

After a while, the Salesians made their way to the center of that huge crowd and knelt down. The savages laid their arms at the feet of the missionaries and knelt down with them to pray. One of the Salesians then intoned the hymn: *Laudate Mariam, O Linguae Fideles*—"Praise Mary, O Faithful Tongues." The savages took up the strain, verse after verse. Such was the volume of their vigorous singing that it frightened me and I awoke.

Now who were those savages?

Don Bosco at first believed that they were the people of Ethiopia, but as soon as he had precise information as to the traits and customs of the Ethiopians, he abandoned the idea. Then he thought that they might be the people of the district around Hong Kong, but when he had spoken to a Chinese missionary who had come to Turin at that time in search of vocations, he knew that these were not the people of his dream.

He then took up the study of the Australian missions, but he was still unable to locate the people of his dream. And when Rome thought of confiding to him a vicariate Apostolic in Australia, his thoughts went back again to the black Aborigines, but still he remained unconvinced.

And when he received more and more pressing invitations from Argentina, he realized clearly, and to the exclusion of all other ideas, that his sons were called to perform their first mission work amongst the wilds of Patagonia and that it was that bare and uninviting country that he had seen in his vision. In the chronicle we read that more and more letters arrived from Argentina for the Feast of St. Francis de Sales, January 29, 1875, and that Don Bosco, surrounded by his council and the various local Superiors on the stage of the theatre of the Oratory, had them read out loud to his boys, for even from the beginning the boys were considered as part of the Salesian family and had to be kept *au courant* of the big events that had a bearing on its destiny. From these letters it was seen that everything was now arranged and that all that had now to be sought was the approval of the Holy Father.

For this purpose Don Bosco went to Rome and had an audience with the Pope. His Holiness entrusted the whole business to Cardinal Franchi and, having heard his report, without further formality or delay approved and blessed the new mission.

N.B. Regarding the First Missionary Expedition consult *Biographical Memoirs*, Vol. XI and Vol. XII (1875).

THE ANGEL OF ARPHAXAD 38
(Second Missionary Dream)

The designs of God on the Salesian Congregation in the remote future, as narrated by Don Bosco to the Superior Council, July 2, 1885.) (*Biographical Memoirs*, Vol. XVII, page 643ff.)

It seemed to me that I was in front of a very high mountain on the top of which stood an Angel, resplendent with such bright light that he illumined the furthermost countries. Around the mountain was a vast kingdom of unknown tribes.

In his right hand, the Angel was holding aloft a sword that shone like a very bright flame, while with the left hand he was pointing out to me the regions all around. He was telling me: *Angelus Arphaxad vocat vos ad proelianda bella Domini et ad congregandos populos in horrea Domini*—"The Angel of Arphaxad[1] calls you to wage the wars of the Lord and to gather the people into the barns of the Lord." His word, however, was not in the form of command, as on the other occasions, but as by way of proposal.

A marvelous crowd of Angels, whose names either I did not know or could not remember, surrounded him. Among them was Louis Colle,[2] around whom stood as a crown a multitude of boys whom he was teaching to sing hymns to God; he too sang with them.

---

1. Arphaxad was the son of Sem and grandson of Noah. (*Gen*. 10:22).
2. Louis Colle was a holy youth who had died a holy death and often used to appear to Don Bosco to reveal secret things to him.

Around the mountain, at its foot and on its slopes, there lived many people. All were talking among themselves, but it was a strange language, and I could not understand it. I could only understand what the Angel said. I cannot describe what I have seen. They are things that one can see, one can understand, but cannot explain. At one and the same time, I could see separate objects simultaneously, which would continually change the spectacle that was before me.

Therefore, now it seemed to me that that was the plain of Mesopotamia, now a very high mountain; and that same mountain on which the Angel of Arphaxad was standing would take a thousand and one aspects every moment, so that the people that lived there seemed but roaming shadows.

In front of this mountain and during all this journey, it seemed to me that I was raised to an immense height, as above the clouds, in an immense space. Who can express in words that height, that breadth, that light, that brightness, that spectacle! A sight that one can enjoy, but that cannot be described!

In this and in the other sights there were many who accompanied me, exhorting me to have courage, and who were also encouraging the Salesians, that they might not stop along the way. Among those who eagerly pulled me, so to say, by the hand, that I might go forward, there was the dear boy Louis Colle and bands of Angels who re-echoed the songs of those boys that surrounded him.

Then it seemed to me that I was in the center of Africa in a very vast desert; there on the ground was written in large transparent letters: *Negroes*. In the middle there stood the Angel of Cham, who kept saying: "*Cessabit maledictum—* 'The curse will cease'—and the Creator's blessing will descend on His reprobate children, and honey and balsam will cure the bites of the snakes; then will be covered the turpitude of the children of Cham." All those people were naked.

And then it seemed to me that I was in Australia. Here too was an Angel who was walking and making people walk toward the South. Australia was not a continent, but an aggregate of many islands, whose inhabitants were all different in character and appearance. A multitude of children that lived there were trying to come toward us, but they were prevented by distance and by the seas that separated them. But they stretched out their hands toward Don Bosco and the Salesians, saying: "Come to our aid! Why don't you complete the work which your fathers have begun?" Many of them halted, but others with incredible efforts crossed among ferocious animals and came and mixed with the Salesians whom I did not know, and they all began to sing: *Benedictus qui venit in nomine Domini!*—"Blessed is he who comes in the name of the Lord!"

At some distance one could see masses of innumerable islands; but I could not make out details of them. It seemed to me that all I saw meant that Divine Providence offered a portion of that evangelical field to the Salesians, but at a future date. Their labors will be fruitful, because the hand of the Lord will constantly be with them, *provided they do not make themselves unworthy of His favors.*

Could I but embalm and preserve alive fifty of the Salesians who are now here with us, in 500 years they would see what stupendous destiny Providence has in store for the Salesians, *if we shall be faithful*!!

Within 150 or 200 years, the Salesians will be masters of the whole world (i.e., leading in all the world)!

We shall always be acceptable even to the wicked ones, because our special field is such that attracts the sympathy and good will of all, good and bad. There may arise some who might want to see us destroyed, but theirs will be isolated attempts and without the support of others.

The condition is that the Salesians be *not caught by the love of comforts and hence avoid work.* Even keeping only the works that we have in hand and not *giving ourselves to the vice of greed*, they will have an assurance, a guarantee, of long duration.

The Salesian Society will prosper materially if we shall make efforts to *sustain and diffuse the Bulletin*, the work of the "*Sons of Mary, Help of Christians,*" and shall promote it. Some of these children are so good! Their institution is the one that will give us valiant confrères, firm in their vocation (late vocations).

These are the things Don Bosco saw more distinctly, that he better remembered and narrated the first time. But later on he spoke to Don Lemoyne of many more things seen in a rapid and passing vision. He saw nations, cities, seas, peoples, islands, habits of peoples, spectacles impossible to describe. It was a circular trip around the southern part of the hemisphere. (Cf. p. 646).

The Angel of Arphaxad: Arphaxad was one of the grandsons of Noah. (*Gen.* 10:22). Following the ethnographical divisions, some say he was the father of the people of Mesopotamia; others instead see in him the father of the peoples of India and China. He was certainly the forefather of some Asiatic race. Don Bosco connected the Angel of Arphaxad with China, and after this vision he often spoke of him in connection with the Salesian missions. He saw in this vision a confirmation of the preceding dreams about the missions. (Cf. Vol. XVII, p. 647.)

THE FUTURE OF THE SALESIAN MISSIONS (Fifth Missionary Dream) 39

(*Biographical Memoirs*, Vol. XVIII, page 72)

On another occasion Don Bosco was given a glimpse of the great things that the future held in store for the Salesian missions. He had gone, in 1886, on a visit to Barcelona, and during his stay of several weeks, had been treated with unlimited kindness, and almost veneration, by large numbers of fervent admirers.

One night it seemed to him that he was wandering aimlessly in the midst of many little woody heights, when all at once he was startled by an uproar that proceeded from a large crowd of children who were running towards him and shouting in rapturous glee: "Here you are at last! We have waited for you for a long time and now we shall not let you go away from us!" Don Bosco stood there confused and uncertain what to do, when there suddenly appeared—as Don Viglietti, to whom Don Bosco recounted the dream, relates—a great flock of sheep in the charge of a shepherd girl. She immediately set to work to arrange all her woolly charges on one side of the space in which they were standing, while the boys were ranged up on the other. Then she turned to Don Bosco and asked: "Do you see all that is here before you?"

"Certainly," said Don Bosco. "I see everything quite plainly."

"Good. And do you remember that dream which you had when almost ten years of age?"

"I cannot recall it at present; my mind is very tired."

"Just think a little and you will soon remember everything," said the Shepherdess.

Then she told Don Bosco and the boys to follow her to one side, and commanded: "Look now from here; look, all of you, and tell me what you see written. What do you see?"

"I see," said Don Bosco, "some mountains and then the sea, then some hills, more mountains and then the sea again."

"And I," said one of the boys, "can see Valparaiso."

"And I," said another, "Santiago."

"And I can read both those words," said a third.

"Well now," continued the Shepherdess, "just start from this point and you will have an idea of how much the Salesians are going to do in the future. Turn around now to this side; draw a line mentally from here and then look again."

"I see mountains, hills and seas!" exclaimed Don Bosco.

The boys also strained their eyes in the direction indicated, and exclaimed in chorus: "We can read Pekin!"

Then Don Bosco beheld a great city through which flowed a wide river, spanned by several bridges.

"Very well," said the maiden, who seemed to be their teacher, "now draw a line from one extremity to the other, that is to say, from Pekin to Santiago; make your line touch a point in the center of Africa, and you will have an exact idea of the work that will be done by the Salesians."

"But," objected Don Bosco, "how can we do so much? The distances are immense; the places indicated are very difficult to reach; and the Salesians are but few."

"Do not trouble yourself about that," rejoined the Shepherdess. "This will all be done by your sons and by your sons' sons. Only let them remain firm in the observance of the Rule and the spirit of the Salesian Society."

"But," continued Don Bosco, "where are all these people to come from?"

"Just come and see. There you have 500 missionaries all ready and willing to work hard. Beyond them you can see more and still more. Just draw a line *from Santiago to the center of Africa,* and now what do you see?"

"I can see," replied Don Bosco, *"ten stations or centers."*

"Very well," said the Shepherdess. *"These centers which you see will be houses of study and novitiates and will in time produce multitudes of missionaries for work in these countries.* And now, just turn around here; here you have *ten more centers* from the middle of Africa to Pekin. These will provide missionaries for the other countries. There you have *Hong Kong, Calcutta* and farther over here *Madagascar.* These and other centers besides will have their houses, houses of study and novitiates."

Don Bosco stood drinking in every word and looking attentively at every point indicated. Then he said again, "But still I don't see where so many people are to come from. And how are the missionaries to be sent to these places? There we have savages who live on human flesh, there we have heretics and pagans—how, in the face of such difficulties, can so much be done?"

"Listen and I shall tell you. Strive always to *have a great good will.* After that there is only one other thing—*to see that my sons cultivate assiduously and constantly Mary's own virtue."*

"I think," said Don Bosco, "that I understand all you have said to me, and I shall preach your counsels everywhere and to all."

"And be on your guard," continued the Blessed Virgin (for that Shepherdess must have been Our Lady herself) "against an error which is now very prevalent: *the tendency among students to mix up the divine and human arts; the science of Heaven should not be mixed with earthly things."*

Don Bosco was on the point of speaking again when the whole vision vanished. His dream was at an end.

"How our Mother Mary loves us!" was Don Bosco's comment when he had finished relating to his Salesians at Barcelona what he had seen.

THE TWO COLUMNS IN THE SEA   **40**

(Biographical Memoirs, Vol. VII, Ch. XVIII, page 169ff.)

On May 14, 1862, Don Bosco had the joy of receiving the first religious professions of twenty-two members of the Salesian Society just constituted.

Then among the rest he told the newly professed that he had sure proofs that the Salesian Society, by God's will, would prosper. And in speaking to them, he manifested an extraordinary satisfaction.

Some days later, on the 30th of May, he narrated the following dream. It concerns the battles of the Church against many adversaries, the sufferings of the Pope and the final triumph through devotion to the Holy Eucharist and to Mary, Help of Christians.

I want to tell you a dream. It is true that he who is dreaming is not reasoning; anyway I, who would even tell you my sins if I were not afraid that they would make you all run away and make the house tumble down, *tell you this for your spiritual profit.* I had the dream some days ago.

The Dream

Imagine yourselves to be with me on the seashore, or better, on an isolated rock and not to see any patch of land other than what is under your feet. On the whole of that vast sheet of water you see an innumerable fleet of ships in battle array. The prows of the ships are formed into sharp, spearlike points so that wherever they are thrust they pierce and completely destroy. These ships are armed with cannons, with lots of rifles, with incendiary materials, with other arms of all kinds, and also with *books*, and they advance against a ship very much bigger and higher than themselves and try to dash against it with the prows or to burn it or in some way to do it every possible harm.

The Ship of the Church

As escorts to that majestic fully equipped ship, there are many smaller ships, which receive commands by signal from it and carry out movements to defend themselves from the opposing fleet.

The Two Columns

In the midst of the immense expanse of sea, two mighty columns of great height arise a little distance the one from the other. On the top of one, there is the statue of the Immaculate Virgin, from whose feet hangs a large placard with this inscription: *Auxilium Christianorum*—"Help of Christians"; on the other, which is much higher and bigger, stands a Host of great size proportionate to the column and beneath is another placard with the words: *Salus Credentium*—"Salvation of the Faithful."

The Holy Father

The supreme commander on the big ship is the Sovereign Pontiff. He, on seeing the fury of the enemies and the evils

John Bosco's famous prophetic dream of The Two Columns in the Sea, which referred to a great battle that would occur in the future between the Church and her enemies.

among which his faithful find themselves, determines to summon around himself the captains of the smaller ships to hold a council and decide on what is to be done.

In Conclave

All the captains come aboard and gather around the Pope. They hold a meeting, but meanwhile the wind and the waves gather in storm, so they are sent back to control their own ships.

There comes a short lull; for a second time the Pope gathers the captains together around him, while the flag-ship goes on its course. But the frightful storm returns.

The Pope stands at the helm and all his energies are directed to steering the ship towards those two columns, from the top of which and from every side of which are hanging numerous anchors and big hooks, fastened to chains.

The Battle

All the enemy ships move to attack it, and they try in every way to stop it and to sink it: some with writings or books or inflammable materials, of which they are full; others with guns, with rifles and with rams. The battle rages ever more relentlessly. The enemy prows thrust violently, but their efforts and impact prove useless. They make attempts in vain and waste all their labor and ammunition; the big ship goes safely and smoothly on its way. Sometimes it happens that, struck by formidable blows, it gets large, deep gaps in its sides; but no sooner is the harm done than a gentle breeze blows from the two columns and the cracks close up and the gaps are stopped immediately.

Destruction of the Enemy

Meanwhile, the guns of the assailants are blown up, the rifles and other arms and prows are broken; many ships are shattered and sink into the sea. Then, the frenzied enemies strive to fight hand to hand, with fists, with blows, with blasphemy and with curses.

All at once the Pope falls gravely wounded. Immediately, those who are with him run to help him and they lift him up. A second time the Pope is struck, he falls again and dies. A shout of victory and of joy rings out amongst the enemies; from their ships an unspeakable mockery arises.

A New Pope

But hardly is the Pontiff dead than another Pope takes his place. The pilots, having met together, have elected the Pope so promptly that the news of the death of the Pope coincides with the news of the election of the successor. The adversaries begin to lose courage.

Haven of Rest

The new Pope, putting the enemy to rout and overcoming every obstacle, guides the ship right up to the two columns and comes to rest between them; he makes it fast with a light chain that hangs from the bow to an anchor of the column on which stands the Host; and with another light chain which hangs from the stern, he fastens it at the opposite end to another anchor hanging from the column on which stands the Immaculate Virgin.

Rout of the Enemy

Then a great convulsion takes place. All the ships that until then had fought against the Pope's ship are scattered; they flee away, collide and break to pieces one against another. Some sink and try to sink others. Several small ships that had fought gallantly for the Pope race to be the first to bind themselves to those two columns.

Many other ships, having retreated through fear of the battle, cautiously watch from far away; the wrecks of the broken ships having been scattered in the whirlpools of the sea, they in their turn sail in good earnest to those two columns, and, having reached them, they make themselves fast to the hooks hanging down from them and there they remain safe, together with the principal ship, on which is the Pope. Over the sea there reigns a great calm.

Don Bosco Explains

At this point Don Bosco asked Don Rua:

"What do you think of the story?"

Don Rua answered: "It seems to me that the Pope's ship might mean the Church, of which he is the head: the ships, men; the sea, this world. Those who defend the big ship are the good, lovingly attached to the Holy See; the others are her enemies, who try with every kind of weapon to annihilate her. The two columns of salvation seem to be devotion to Mary Most Holy and to the Blessed Sacrament of the Eucharist."

Don Rua did not speak of the Pope who fell and died, and Don Bosco also was silent about him. He simply added: "You are right! Only I ought to correct one expression. The enemy ships are persecutions. The most serious trials for the Church are near at hand. That which has been so far is almost nothing in the face of that which must befall. Her enemies are represented by the ships that tried to sink the principal ship if they could. Only two means are left to save her amidst so much confusion: DEVOTION TO MARY MOST HOLY and FREQUENT COMMUNION, making use of every means and doing our best to practice them and having them practiced everywhere and by everybody."

(Don Bosco did not give any other explanations.)

A LETTER WRITTEN BY
ST. JOHN BOSCO
ON EDUCATION

(*Biographical Memoirs*, Vol. XVII, Ch. III)

This writing is a treasure, which, together with the short treatise on the Preventive System and the Regulations for the Salesian Houses, form the Pedagogical trilogy left by Don Bosco as a heritage for his sons. It is a pedagogy at once simple and sublime, which, when well understood and well carried out, can make of institutes of education places of joy, havens of innocence, hearths of virtue, centers of study, nurseries of excellent Christians, of good citizens and of worthy ecclesiastics. Good will and sacrifice, however, are very necessary.   —D. Ceria

My dear Sons in Jesus Christ,

Whether I am near you or far away, you are always the object of my thoughts. My one desire is to see you happy in time and in eternity; and it is this thought, this desire, which determined me to write this letter to you. Being far away from you, my dear boys, is a very heavy burden for me, and you cannot imagine the pain it causes me not being able to see you and hear you.

That is why I would have liked to write these lines to you a week ago, but my constant occupations prevented me from doing so. Anyway, though only a few days remain before my return, I want to anticipate my coming among you, and since

I cannot do so in person, it must be by letter. These words of mine are the words of one who loves you tenderly in Jesus Christ, of one who has a duty to speak to you, with the freedom of a father. You, I know, will let me do so, won't you? And you will listen to what I have to say and put it into practice.

Dream—The Oratory Before 1870

I have said that you are the only constant object of my thoughts. Well, then, a few evenings ago I had retired to my room, and while I was preparing for bed, I began saying the prayers which my good mother taught me.

Then I am not sure whether I was overcome by sleep or distracted—I seemed to be standing before two of the past pupils of the Oratory. One of the two came up to me and, after greeting me affectionately, said:

"Don Bosco, do you know me?"

"Of course I know you," I replied.

"And you still remember me?" he continued.

"I remember you and all the others; you are Valfrè, and you were in the Oratory before 1870."

"Tell me," he continued, "would you like to see the boys who were in the Oratory in my time?"

"Oh yes! let me see them," I replied. That would give me great pleasure."

The Vision of the Past

Valfrè then showed me the boys just as they were in those days—the same in appearance, height and age. I seemed to be in the old Oratory during recreation: it was a lively scene—all movement and joy. Some were running, some jumping or getting others to jump; here they were playing leap-frog, there bararotta or football. In one spot there was a group of boys listening carefully to a Priest who was telling them a story; elsewhere, there was a Brother in the middle of a group of boys playing games of forfeit with them. There was song and laughter from all sides; Priests and Brothers were everywhere, and around them the boys were romping merrily. It was obvious that the greatest cordiality and confidence existed between the boys and their Superiors. I was charmed at all this, and Valfrè said to me: "You see, affability brings affection and confidence: this is what opens the hearts of the boys, and they manifest everything without the slightest fear to their teachers, assistants and Superiors. They become sincere in Confession and outside, and they are docile to all that is commanded them by their Superior, of whose love for them they are fully assured.

The Great Contrast

At that moment the other past pupil—who had a white beard, drew near me and said: "Don Bosco, would you like to see and know the boys who are in the Oratory at present?" "Yes," I replied, "it's a month since I have seen them." And so Joseph Buzzetti showed them to me. I saw the Oratory and all of you in recreation, but no longer were there joyful shouts and songs, no longer all that lively activity of the first scene.

You could see dissatisfaction in the actions and on the faces of many boys—a weariness, dejection and mistrust that pained my heart. True enough, I did see many boys running and playing about in completely carefree fashion; but many others I saw standing alone, leaning against pillars, buried in desolate thoughts; still others were on the stairways and in the corridors or on the balconies facing the garden, so as to avoid the common recreation. There were some others strolling about in groups, talking in low tones among themselves, casting nervous and ill-meaning glances about, smiling occasionally; but with the smile went a malignant look, which made one convinced without a doubt that St. Aloysius would have blushed to find himself in such company. And even among those who did join in the games, there were some who played so reluctantly as to make it quite plain that they derived no enjoyment from their recreation.

"Do you see your boys?" the past pupil asked.

"Yes," I sighed.

"How very different from what we were once!" he exclaimed.

"Alas, yes! What a lack of enthusiasm in this recreation!"

And that is why many are cold in their approach to the Sacraments; it causes their neglect of the practices of piety in church and elsewhere, and their reluctance to stay in the place where Divine Providence showers on them all that is good for their body, soul and intellect. Hence it is that many do not correspond to their vocation; so, too, their ingratitude towards Superiors, as well as their sly behavior and grumbling, with all their deplorable consequences.

The Remedy

"Yes, I see," I answered. "But how can I get my boys to revive their former vivacity, joyfulness and frankness?"

"With charity!"

"With charity? But are my boys not loved sufficiently? You know that I love them. You know how much I had to put up with on their account for forty years now, and how much I still suffer even now. What privations, how many humiliations, how much opposition and persecution in order that they should have food and shelter, that they should have teachers, and above all that their spiritual welfare should be provided for. I have done everything I possibly could for my boys; they are the apple of my eye."

"I was not speaking about you."

"Of whom then do you speak? Of those who take my place? The rectors, prefects, teachers and assistants? Do you not see that they are martyrs of duty and study? See how they spend the years of their youth for those whom Divine Providence has confided to them!"

"Yes, I know that. But it is not enough—something better still is wanting."

"And what is that?"

"It is not enough that the boys should be loved: they themselves must know they are loved."

"But haven't they eyes in their heads? Haven't they intelligence? Do they not see that all that is done for them is done for love of them?"

"No; I repeat, that is not enough."

"Well, then, what is required of us?"

"This: that by satisfying them in the things they like, by the participation in their boyish inclinations, they will learn to see your love for them in those things which they naturally dislike, such things as discipline, study and self-mortification; and they will learn to do these things with pleasure and love."

"I don't quite follow."

"Have a look at the boys in recreation."

I looked and then rejoined: "What is there to see that is so very special?"

"Do you not understand after all these years educating boys?"

"Look more carefully. Where are our Salesians?"

I looked, and noticed that very few Priests and Brothers were mixing with the boys, and fewer still were taking part in their games. No longer were the Superiors the soul of the recreation. The majority of them were walking and conversing together without any care of what the pupils were doing; others were watching the games, without a thought for the boys; others again were supervising from a distance, without noticing many little disorders, while some did take notice, but in a threatening manner, and even then only rarely. There were some Salesians who would have liked to join some groups of boys, but I saw that those boys did their best to get far away from their teachers and Superiors. Then my friend said:

"In the old days of the Oratory, were you not always among the boys, especially at recreations? Do you remember those grand years? It was a little bit of Heaven, a time that we always recall with love, because love was the rule of our lives and we kept no secrets from you."

"Yes, indeed. And then everything was a joy to me; the boys liked to come to me to hear me speaking, and they had a lively desire of receiving my advice and acting on it. But now you see how I am kept from them by continual visits and occupations and by my poor health."

"Very well; but if you cannot do it, then why do your Salesians not imitate you? Why do you not insist, demand, that they treat the boys as you treated them?"

"I speak until I am hoarse, but unfortunately many do not feel themselves able to stand the strain as we did."

"And so they neglected your simple method and then come to lose the fruit of their labors. Let them love what the boys like, and the boys will come to love what the Superiors like, and this will make their work easy. In the olden days hearts were open to the Superiors, and the boys loved and obeyed them; but now the Superiors are regarded as Superiors and no longer as fathers, brothers and friends, and therefore they are feared and not loved. So if you want that all should be of one heart and soul again, for the love of Jesus, that fatal barrier of mistrust must be removed, and filial confidence must take its place. Then let obedience lead the pupils as a mother leads her child, and peace and joy will reign once more at the Oratory."

"But how are we to remove this barrier?"

"Familiarity with the boys, especially during recreations. Without familiarity no love can be shown, and without this manifestation of love there can be no confidence. He who wishes to be loved must first show his love. Jesus Christ, in dealing with the little ones, became as one of them, and He took our infirmities upon Himself. He is our example in famil-

"The Saving Raft: War on Sin." This picture symbolizes St. John Bosco's protection of his boys amidst the turmoil of worldly temptations.

iarity. The teacher who is seen only in the classroom, and nowhere else, is a teacher and nothing more; but let him go with his boys to recreation and he becomes a brother.

"If one is seen only preaching from the pulpit, it can be said he is doing only what is his strict duty; but let him drop a good word in recreation, and that is the word of a loving heart. How many conversions were brought about by those few spontaneous words of yours whispered in a boy's ear while he was engrossed in his games! If a boy knows he is loved, he will love in return; and if the Superior is loved, he can get everything—especially from boys. This confidence creates an electric current between the boys and their Superiors; the boys' hearts open, their needs are known and their sentiments disclosed. This confidence makes the task lighter, and by it the ingratitude, the troubles, the faults and the failings of the boys become bearable.

"Jesus Christ did not crush the bruised reed nor quench the smoking flax. There is your model! And so nobody will be seen working for vainglory; nobody punishing merely to vindicate wounded self-love; nobody avoiding assisting the boys through a jealous fear of another's popularity; nobody criticizing his confreres with a view to obtaining the boys' love and esteem exclusively for himself—while gaining nothing in fact but the boys' contempt and maybe a lying smile. You will find nobody then allowing his heart to be captured by any boy and neglecting the others in order to attend to him; nobody shirking his bounden duty of vigilance through a love of ease and comfort, or refraining through human respect from admonishing when admonition is called for.

"If this love reigns, all will seek only the glory of God and the salvation of souls. It is when this love cools down that things begin to go wrong. Why do you want to replace charity with the rigidity of a few rules? Why do Superiors avoid the observance of those rules of education which you have laid down for them? Why is it that for the system of loving and preventive vigilance there is being substituted a system of framing rules—a system that is less burdensome and more convenient for the Superior? If the rules are enforced by punishment, they enkindle hatred and give rise to unpleasantness; whereas, if their observance is not enforced, they engender contempt for the Superiors and cause serious disorders.

"This is bound to happen where there is no family spirit. So then, if you want those old happy days to return to the Oratory, let the old system be practiced again. Let the Superior be all things to everyone, always ready to hear any complaint or doubts of the boys, using a paternal vigilance over their conduct; and let his heart be set on seeking the spiritual and temporal welfare of those whom Providence has confided to him. Then the boys' hearts will open; then that air of secrecy and deadly tendency of hiding everything will disappear. Only in matters of scandal let the Superior be inexorable: better run the risk of sending away an innocent boy than keep one who is a cause of scandal. Assistants must consider it a strict obligation in conscience to make known to the Superior everything that may in any way be an offense against God!"

Then I asked him: "Which is the best means to see that familiarity, love and confidence flourish among us once more?

"The exact observance of the Rules of the House."

"Nothing else?"

"The best appetizer in a dinner is the smiling face of those about you."

As my old friend was bringing the conversation to a close, with a heavy heart I kept on watching that lifeless recreation; but little by little I felt exhausted and weighed down by a sense of oppression, which went on increasing to such an extent that I came to myself. I found I was standing by my bed. My legs were so stiff and painful that I could no longer stand. It was already too late. I therefore went to bed determined to write these lines to my boys.

I wish not to have these dreams, because they leave me completely exhausted. Throughout the following day, I felt exceedingly weak and I longed for the night to come that I might have a calm, sound sleep. But as soon as I was in bed, the dream began again. Before me I had the playground, the present Oratory boys and the same past pupil of the Oratory, whom I began to question again at once:

"I will not fail to inform the Salesians of all that you told me, but what shall I tell the Oratory boys?"

"Tell them," he said, "that they should realize all the Superiors, masters and assistants do for them and how much they work for their sakes; if it were not for their love they would never subject themselves to so many sacrifices. Remind them that humility is the source of all happiness; tell them to bear defects of others, for perfection is not to be found in this world. It is a thing of Paradise. They must stop all kinds of grumblings which freeze the heart. Above all, tell them that their main efforts must be to live in God's grace. Whosoever is not at peace with God is not at peace with himself or with others."

"Do you tell me, then, that there are some of my boys who are not in the state of grace?"

"This is the main cause of this lamentable state of affairs—this and others of which you are aware without my mentioning them, and which you must remedy. Only he who has some secrets mistrusts others, for he is always afraid lest these secrets become known, and he is fully aware that if they should become public he would be covered with shame and confusion. Besides that, if his heart is not at peace with God, he will be uneasy and troubled, intolerant of obedience, easily upset over nothing at all; everything seems to be against him, and as he himself feels no love, he will draw the conclusion that the Superiors do not love him."

"And yet how many of the boys daily frequent the Sacraments of Confession and Communion!"

"True enough; many do go to Confession, but what is absolutely lacking is firmness in their resolutions. They go to Confession, but they always bring the same faults, the same occasions of sin, the same bad habits, the same acts of disobedience and neglect of duty. And they go on like this month after month, and even for years; some carry on like that even to the end of their school days. These Confessions are worth little or nothing, and so no peace of soul is obtained from them; and if a boy were to be called in such a state before the judgment seat of God, it would be a serious matter indeed."

"Are there many like that in the Oratory?"

"No, considering the great number of boys you have in the House, they are not many. Look at them." And he pointed them out to me. I watched and saw those boys, one by one. But in those few boys I noticed things that deeply saddened my heart. I do not want to write them on paper, but when I return I want to explain to each of those concerned. For the time being, I will only tell you to pray and to make firm resolutions, showing by your behavior that you are in earnest, and see to it that Comollos, the Dominic Savios, the Besuccos and the Saccardis live in our midst again. As a final word to my friend, I asked: "Have you anything else to tell me?"

"Tell all, young and old, that they are the sons of Mary, Help of Christians," he said, "that she has brought them here to protect them from the dangers of the world, so that they may love one another as brothers and give glory to God and to her by their good conduct. Tell them that it is Our Lady who, by an endless stream of favors and graces, provides for them bread and all that they need for their studies. Let them remember that they are on the threshold of their Holy Mother's feast day, and that it is with her help that that barrier must fall—the barrier of mistrust that the devil has so cunningly raised between Superiors and boys in order to use it as a means for the ruin of certain souls."

"And shall we succeed in removing the barrier?"

"Assuredly," he replied, "if only young and old are ready to suffer some little mortification for the love of Mary, and if they put into practice what I have told you."

Meanwhile, I continued to look at my boys, and at the sight of those whom I saw heading for their eternal perdition my heart was so pained that I awoke. I should like to tell you very many more things which are also of great importance, but I have neither the time nor the opportunity now.

A picture illustrating the fact that the secret of St. John Bosco's success was his singular devotion to the Blessed Virgin Mary.

I now leave you. Do you know the only desire of this old man who has spent his life for his dear boys? Nothing else but that, as far as possible, the happy days of the old Oratory may return: the days of affection and Christian confidence between the boys and the Superiors; the days of condescension and mutual forbearance for the love of Jesus Christ; the days when hearts were open in all simplicity and candor, the days of charity and true happiness for all.

I need the consolation of your promise that you will do all I ask of you for the good of your soul. You do not sufficiently realize the great good fortune that is yours in being sheltered in the Oratory. Before God, I assure you that it is enough for a boy to enter a Salesian House and the Blessed Virgin at once takes him under her special protection. Let us therefore be of one mind. Charity on the part of those who command, charity on the part of those who obey; and the result will be the spirit of St. Francis de Sales reigning in our midst.

My dear boys, the time is drawing near when I must part from you and go into eternity, so I have an ardent desire of leaving you Priests, Brothers and dear boys on that path which the Lord Himself desires for you.

For this end, the Holy Father, whom I saw on Friday, May 9, with all his heart sends you his blessings. The Feast of Mary, Help of Christians, will find me back with you before the picture of our Most Holy Mother. I want this feast day to be kept with the greatest possible solemnity. I leave it to Fr. Lazzero and Fr. Marchisio to solemnize it also in the refectory. The Feast of Mary, Help of Christians, must be a prelude to that everlasting feast we shall celebrate together one day in Heaven.

Rome, May 10, 1884

Yours most affectionately in Jesus Christ,
FR. JOHN BOSCO

A NOTE
FOR THE
SALESIANS

Here are some special monitory dream-visions very important for the Salesians.

From the *Biographical Memoirs:*

At a glance: THE BIOGRAPHICAL MEMOIRS OF SAINT JOHN BOSCO.
The references are to the original Italian edition.

Volume	Period	Pages	Dreams	Author	Printed in
I	1815-41	547	10	G. Lemoyne	1898
II	1841-47	597	6	G. Lemoyne	1901
III	1847-49	663	4	G. Lemoyne	1903
IV	1850-54	766	—	G. Lemoyne	1904
V	1854-58	953	9	G. Lemoyne	1905
VI	1858-61	1,102	17	G. Lemoyne	1907
VII	1862-64	931	15	G. Lemoyne	1909
VIII	1865-67	1,110	12	G. Lemoyne	1912
IX	1868-70	1,032	17	G. Lemoyne	1917
X	1871-74	1,389	17	A. Amadei	1939
XI	1875	627	5	E. Ceria	1930
XII	1876	714	9	E. Ceria	1931
XIII	1877-78	1,021	6	E. Ceria	1932
XIV	1879-80	859	6	E. Ceria	1933
XV	1881-82	882	6	E. Ceria	1933
XVI	1883	735	2	E. Ceria	1935
XVII	1884-85	920	20	E. Ceria	1935
XVIII	1886-88	897	21	E. Ceria	1937
XIX	1888-1938	454	—	E. Ceria	1939
XX	Anal. Index	620	—	E. Foglio	1948
20 vols.	72 yrs., 5 mos., 15 days	16,830	179	4	50 yr. period

If you have enjoyed this book, consider making your next selection from among the following . . .

Prices subject to change.

Visits to the Blessed Sacrament. *St. Alphonsus* 5.00
Moments Divine—Before the Blessed Sacrament. *Reuter* 10.00
Miraculous Images of Our Lady. *Cruz* 21.50
Miraculous Images of Our Lord. *Cruz* 16.50
Raised from the Dead. *Fr. Hebert* 18.50
Love and Service of God, Infinite Love. *Mother Louise Margaret* 15.00
Life and Work of Mother Louise Margaret. *Fr. O'Connell* 15.00
Autobiography of St. Margaret Mary. 7.50
Thoughts and Sayings of St. Margaret Mary 6.00
The Voice of the Saints. *Comp. by Francis Johnston* 8.00
The 12 Steps to Holiness and Salvation. *St. Alphonsus* 9.00
The Rosary and the Crisis of Faith. *Cirrincione & Nelson* 2.00
Sin and Its Consequences. *Cardinal Manning* 9.00
St. Francis of Paola. *Simi & Segreti* 9.00
Dialogue of St. Catherine of Siena. *Transl. Algar Thorold* 12.50
Catholic Answer to Jehovah's Witnesses. *D'Angelo* 13.50
Twelve Promises of the Sacred Heart. (100 cards). 5.00
Life of St. Aloysius Gonzaga. *Fr. Meschler* 13.00
The Love of Mary. *D. Roberto* 9.00
Begone Satan. *Fr. Vogl*. 4.00
The Prophets and Our Times. *Fr. R. G. Culleton* 15.00
St. Therese, The Little Flower. *John Beevers* 7.50
St. Joseph of Copertino. *Fr. Angelo Pastrovicchi* 8.00
Mary, The Second Eve. *Cardinal Newman* 4.00
Devotion to Infant Jesus of Prague. *Booklet* 1.50
Reign of Christ the King in Public & Private Life. *Davies* 2.00
The Wonder of Guadalupe. *Francis Johnston* 9.00
Apologetics. *Msgr. Paul Glenn*. 12.50
Baltimore Catechism No. 1 . . . . 5.00
Baltimore Catechism No. 2 . . . . 7.00
Baltimore Catechism No. 3 . . . . 11.00
An Explanation of the Baltimore Catechism. *Fr. Kinkead*. 18.00
Bethlehem. *Fr. Faber* 20.00
Bible History. *Schuster* 16.50
Blessed Eucharist. *Fr. Mueller* 10.00
Catholic Catechism. *Fr. Faerber* 9.00
The Devil. *Fr. Delaporte* 8.50
Dogmatic Theology for the Laity. *Fr. Premm* 21.50
Evidence of Satan in the Modern World. *Cristiani* 14.00
Fifteen Promises of Mary. (100 cards). 5.00
Life of Anne Catherine Emmerich. 2 vols. *Schmoeger* 48.00
Life of the Blessed Virgin Mary. *Emmerich* 18.00
Manual of Practical Devotion to St. Joseph. *Patrignani* 17.50
Prayer to St. Michael. (100 leaflets) 5.00
Prayerbook of Favorite Litanies. *Fr. Hebert* 12.50
Preparation for Death. (Abridged). *St. Alphonsus* 12.00
Purgatory Explained. *Schouppe* 16.50
Purgatory Explained. (pocket, unabr.). *Schouppe* 12.00
Fundamentals of Catholic Dogma. *Ludwig Ott* 27.50
Spiritual Conferences. *Faber* 18.00
Trustful Surrender to Divine Providence. *Bl. Claude* 7.00
Wife, Mother and Mystic. *Bessieres* 10.00
The Agony of Jesus. *Padre Pio* 3.00

Prices subject to change.

Prices subject to change.

Prices subject to change.

At your Bookdealer or direct from the Publisher.

Toll-Free 1-800-437-5876   *Fax 815-226-7770*

Prices subject to change.